HASIDISM AND MODERN MAN

Human

God

p. 22 Sacred

p. 22 Profane

Holy/H

Hallowing

p. 39 Hasid = pious man

HASIDISM AND MODERN MAN

MARTIN BUBER

edited and translated by
Maurice Friedman

New Introduction by

Martin S. Jaffee
The Henry M. Jackson School of
International Studies, University of
Washington

an imprint of Prometheus Books
59 John Glenn Drive, Amherst, New York 14228-2197

Published 2000 by Humanity Books, an imprint of Prometheus Books

Inquiries should be addressed to Humanity Books, 59 John Glenn Drive, Amherst, New York 14228–2197. VOICE: 716–691–0133, ext. 207. FAX: 716–564–2711.

04 03   6 5 4 3

Library of Congress Cataloging-in-Publication Data

Buber, Martin, 1878–1965.
Hasidism and modern man / Martin Buber: edited and translated by Maurice Friedman ; with a new introduction by Martin S. Jaffee.
p. cm.
Reprint. Originally published: New York : Horizon Press, 1958. Originally published, with a new introduction : Atlantic Highlands, NJ : Humanities Press International, Inc., 1988.
ISBN 1–57392–460–1 (pbk.)
1. Hasidism. I. Title.
BM198.B793 1988
296.8'33—dc19   87–22907
CIP

Printed in the United States of America on acid-free paper

CONTENTS

INTRODUCTION TO THE SECOND EDITION

The present volume, first compiled in 1958 by Maurice Friedman, brings together a representative sampling of Martin Buber's voluminous writings on Hasidism. When supplemented by the companion volume, *The Origin and Meaning of Hasidism*, compiled by Friedman in 1960, the reader possesses the fundamental outlines of Buber's thought on this remarkable movement of Eastern European Jewish spirituality.[1] Indeed, it is no exaggeration at all to point out that insofar as the educated reader might know something of Hasidism, this knowledge has its likely origins in one of Buber's writings. So, before us is a slim volume, but one which in context constitutes part of an important moment in the West's self-opening to cultures shaped beyond the boundaries of the Greco-Christian tradition.

Buber himself was quite self-conscious of his own role in fostering Western recognition of such cultures. Some of his earliest publishing ventures included interpretive renderings of Asian religious texts, seeking within them a wisdom which, in his view, had been repressed by the dominant traditions of Western civilization. To a great extent, Buber's much larger attention to sources stemming from the Judaic tradition was motivated by a similar interest, for in his earliest writings Judaism was itself portrayed as a spiritual phenomenon of the Orient from which the Christian (or post-Christian) West had much to learn.

INTRODUCTION TO THE SECOND EDITION

In an early lecture on "Judaism and Mankind" (c. 1910), delivered in the conviction that the renewal of the Western spirit lay in the appropriation of Asian models of mystical unification, Buber identified the essence of Judaism as an effort to "evolve unity out of the division of the world."[2] "This", he argued, "is the primal process within the Jew, the process manifested in their personal lives with all the forcefulness of their Asiatic genius by those great Jews in whom the most profound Judaism came alive: unification of the soul. In those Jews the great idea of Asia became exemplary for the Occident—the Asia of boundlessness and of holy unity, the Asia of Lao-Tse and of Buddha, which is the Asia of Moses and of the Isaiahs, of Jesus and of Paul."[3] While the "Oriental" character of Judaism ceased to be a prominent theme in Buber's more mature writings, he remained convinced throughout his life that the Judaic tradition contained truths of the spirit that secular Western culture could ignore only at its own peril.

Buber's self-understanding as a mediator to the West of submerged traditions of redemptive wisdom helps us to appreciate the argument constituted by the essay after which the present volume is named. The juxtaposition of "Hasidism" and "Modern Man" suggests that this apparently parochial creation of a Jewry almost entirely unaffected by modern European thought can genuinely instruct a Europe convinced that its scientific and technological achievement had brought it to the pinnacle of human evolution. There is, of course, an intentional irony here which must not be glossed over. Precisely within that segment of humanity regarding itself as having the greatest mastery of its destiny, as having through the application of technical expertise overcome the fundamental constraints of the human condition—precisely here is the human soul in greatest jeopardy. Among the "primitives," however—precisely that great majority of humanity subjected politically and economically by the West's achievement—the West may yet find the wisdom it requires to resuscitate its waning power to sustain the human spirit.

Buber's Hasidic writings constitute his attempt to present the West with such an alternative wisdom, a wisdom characterized in particular by the creation of a life in which the fragmented elements of personal existence are brought together in unity through the creation of genuine community. In Hasidism, at the ragged Eastern frontier of Western secularism, among a "backward" sect of Polish Jews, Buber proposed to find an image of genuine humanity that the fallen West might emulate. Striking a theme characteristic of most of his Hasidic works, Buber wrote in "My Way to Hasidism" (written in 1918, and included in the present volume, p. 50):

> Hasidism took the social form of a great popular community . . . in all its medley, in all its spiritual and social multiplicity. Never yet in Europe has such a community thus established the whole of life as a unity on the basis of the inwardly known. Here is no separation between faith and work, between

truth and verification, or, in the language of today, between morality and politics; here all is one kingdom, one spirit, one reality.

As, a century earlier, the Evangelical theologian Friedrich Schleiermacher began the theological critique of the Enlightenment with his defense of religion before its "cultivated despisers," Buber now sought to mount an even more penetrating critique of modern culture by presenting the most contemned form of religion in the West—Judaism, whose pristine expression was embodied for Buber in Hasidism—as a principal model of the redeemed life.

It would be an oversimplification, of course, to view Buber's Hasidic works solely as a rhetorical strategy designed to command for Judaism the attention of intellectually serious Europeans. In fact, Buber first emerges as a public figure precisely as a Jew engaging other Jews in discourse on the particular problematic of Jewish spirituality in the age of the West's decline.

Buber's fame as an interpreter of Hasidism, which began with his publication in 1906 of *The Tales of Rabbi Nachman*, had been preceded by earlier renown as a brilliant proponent, among German-Jewish youth, of Zionism, the movement of Jewish national regeneration founded by Theodor Herzl in 1897. Some observations on the nature of Buber's Zionism, which he viewed as a cure for the deracinated Jewish soul mired in the rootless secularism of Western modernity, will be useful in understanding the precise picture of Hasidism which comes to us in Buber's work.

Buber belonged to a generation of young Central European Jews for whom the great promise of Jewish integration into European culture, symbolized by the nineteenth-century fight for Jewish civil rights, had become, at the moment of its full achievement, empty and barren. In its passion for "Europeanization," for demonstrating its entitlement to full political and social participation in European culture, Western Jewry had, like the biblical Esau, sold its most precious birthright for a thin gruel, in this case, bourgeois respectability. To the extent that the Jews had become "modern Europeans," they had adopted a culture that had already begun to reveal its incapacity to sustain the spirit. At the same time, they had abandoned all natural connection to the rich spiritual heritage created by biblical Jewry and transmitted—often by means of subterranean media of esoteric tradition[4]—to subsequent generations throughout the millennia of Exile. Buber saw in Zionism nothing less than the eruption, in a distinctly modern idiom, of powers of spirit that had in antiquity transformed the Israelite people from a fractious mob of slaves into a community where the presence of God brought each person into living relation with the ground of freedom.

In his Zionist writings prior to World War One, while developing in other contexts his thought on the nature of Hasidism, Buber held that a central barrier to the renewal of modern Jewish spirituality lay in Western Jewry's imitative efforts to modernize Judaism through what he termed "a pale, feeble attempt at reform, which derived its thinking and its patterns from the catalogues of European enlightenment and the so-called progressive religions."[5] Buber's objection to religious reform along Western models—at least in this early period of his thought—is that the attempt to ape Western forms of religion constitutes a fundamental denial of Judaism's Oriental spirit, the very source of its power. It is Zionism's practical call for a geographical return of the Jews to their home in Palestine that Buber interpreted in a distinctly historiosophical vein as a movement of the Jewish soul turning back to the distinctive source of its vision in the Orient.[6] Bypassing the inauthentic religiosity of religious reform, Zionism made it possible for Jews to re-engage, as modern men and women, the mode of openness to the holy to which the Jewish Bible so amply testifies.

The lengthy passage which follows, delivered as a speech in 1912, is a crucial text for understanding not only what the early Buber saw in Zionism, but also for grasping how, in his mind, Hasidism constituted a phenomenon of deep relevance to the Zionist attempt to return Jewry to its geographical and spiritual home. Speaking of models by which Jews might liberate themselves from false imitation of the West's institutional religion, Buber observes:[7]

> We need only to look at the decadent yet still wondrous Hasid of our days; to watch him as he prays to his God, shaken by his fervor, expressing

with his whole body what his lips are saying—a sight both grotesque and sublime; to observe him at the close of the Sabbath as he partakes, with kingly gestures and in concentrated dedication, of the sacred meal . . . , and we will feel: here, stunted and distorted yet unmistakable, is Asiatic strength and Asiatic inwardness. On this manifest or latent Orientalism, this base of the Jew's soul that has endured underneath all influences, I build my faith in a new spiritual-religious creation by Judaism. . . . One may undertake bold spiritual ventures, or coin strong spiritual expressions; religious excitement may flash from the storm-heavy darkness of the people's fate; but a great creation that fuses all this into a single synthesis, re-establishes the community of Jewish becoming, and once more gives full expression to the immortal Jewish unitary drive—this will come into being only after the continuity of life in Palestine, where the great concepts of this unitary drive once originated, has been re-established. The Jew is not the same person he once was; he has passed through every heaven and hell of the Occident, and his soul has come to grief. But his original strength has remained unimpaired; indeed, it has been purified. Once it comes into contact with its maternal soil, it will once more become creative. The Jew can truly fulfill his vocation among the nations only when he begins anew, and, with his whole . . . strength, translates into reality what his religion taught him in antiquity: rootedness in his native land; leading the good life within narrow

> confines; and building a model community on the scanty Canaanite soil.

I have already pointed out that Buber later came to view Judaism as less an "Oriental" than a universally human posture of spirit. He grew as well far less sanguine that the modern reunification of the Judaic spirit would somehow automatically take root in the Jewish communal settlements in the Land of Israel. But for our purposes it is the coupling of Hasidism and Zionism which is of interest. For throughout his life Buber would continue to see in each testimony to the same primal Jewish spirit that had been bequeathed to the world in the Hebrew Scriptures.[8]

Echoing the early Zionist theorist, Moses Hess, Buber tells us in "My Way to Hasidism" (48–49), that Hasidism "forms within the living Jewish spirit the transition 'from medieval Judaism to a regenerated Judaism which is only in formation'." "Still bound to the medieval in its outward appearance", Buber continues, "Hasidic Judaism is already open to regeneration in its inner truth, and the degeneration of this great religious movement can only halt but not stop entirely the process in the history of the spirit that began with it." Hasidism, that is, initiating a dialectical movement of the modern Jewish spirit, transcends the historical and social context of its original appearance and continues to reverberate in the soul of the Jewish people in the unanticipated form of the return of secularized Jews to Zion.

While, in his writings after the First World War,

Buber provides Hasidism with greater universalist ramifications (27), this coincides with a similar tendency to focus on Zionism itself as a universalist humanism, distinctive to the needs of Jewry, but presenting all humanity with a model of community in which each member is present wholly to the other, and the community is as a whole open to the presence of the Divine.[9] It is, then, hardly a misrepresentation to claim that, in Buber's lexicon, Hasidism stands as an early-modern embodiment of Judaism's primal truth in a form appropriate to the situation of Israel in its Exile, while Zionism constitutes—when it is genuine to its own genius—a reemergence of that truth in the midst of a Jewish community able and willing to establish anew its common life on its ancestral soil. Hasidism, in other words, is the historical prefiguring of a power of spirit that would achieve its contemporary manifestation in Zionism.

It is crucial to stress, however, that Hasidism remains for Buber the touchstone against which the value of Zionist activity must be tested. For Zionism, precisely because it is a secularist movement engaged in the politics of the power struggle, is in perpetual danger of forgetting what a-political Hasidism always recognized—that redemption in any significant sense depends upon human acts in which the love of God ("religion") and the love of man ("ethics") are fused into one (see "Love of God and Love of Neighbor", p. 233). For Buber, then, Zionism is in critical need of Hasidism's discovery of "an inner tie with the world, with the soul, and with God," for "only through such a contact will it be possible to guard Zionism against following the way of the nationalism of our age, which, by demolishing the bridges which connect it with the world, is destroying its own value and its right to exist."[10]

With the context of Buber's presentation of Hasidism in hand, it is now possible to reflect upon the actual image of Hasidism that we find in writings such as the volume before us. Perhaps the most important observation to make at the outset—especially in light of the trenchant critique of Buber's Hasidic studies by Gershom Scholem, who pioneered the academic study of Jewish mysticism[11]—is that at no point in his work does Buber claim that the Hasidism he presents to his readers is either congruent with contemporary Hasidic life or, indeed, a complete picture of classical Hasidism in its full historical totality. Let us now spell out the premises and implications of Buber's position.

The reader will already have noted in some of the previous citations that Buber tends to dismiss the Hasidism of his own day as a kind of relic that perpetuates the form of Hasidism at the expense of its essence (47–48). This is no casual bias of Buber's, but rather is central to his conception of Hasidism's significance for contemporary spirituality. Insofar as Hasidism has a redemptive role to play in the transformation of the modern soul, it is as an ever-available model of a personal stance in the world, capable of restoring our capacity to enter into relations of genuine mutuality (27). But moderns can take up this stance only in the midst of their own lives in secular modernity, not by imitating the outward appearances of the Hasidic lifestyle or even its pattern of daily life, grounded as they are in cultural and intellectual perspectives from which the modern temper is, as far as Buber is concerned, irretrievably alienated. As Buber admits in his autobiographical reflections below (24), "It would have been an unpermissible masquerading had I taken on the Hasidic manner of life—I who had a wholly other relation to Jewish tradition. . . . It was necessary, rather, to take into my own existence as much as I actually could of what had been truly exemplified for me there, that is to say, of the realization of that dialogue with being whose possibility my thought had shown me."

Buber acknowledges, then, that his depiction of Hasidism is guided not by any desire to present an academic depiction of the Hasidic community as a sociological phenomenon in historical context. Rather, his intention is to mediate an *experience* of Hasidism that is shaped by immersion in Hasidic texts, to restore those elements of Hasidic spirituality that resonate with his own imagination. His stance as an interpreter of Hasidism, in other words, is entirely that of the existentially engaged seeker, for whom knowledge has value only insofar as it facilitates the transformation of the person through the act of knowing. "To know," Buber explains below, "by this I do not mean a storing up of anthropological . . . knowledge . . . ; I mean the immediate knowing, the eye-to-eye knowing of the people in its creative primal hours" ("My Way to Hasidism," p. 58).

For this reason, Buber's presentation of Hasidic texts in translation, as well as his studies of Hasidic thought, focus upon a distinct genre of Hasidic literature—the narrative or folk tale—and a circumscribed period in the history of Hasidism—the first five or six generations up to the middle of the nineteenth century. Buber found precisely here, in a literary genre believed to be close to "the folk," told by generations in more or less living connection with Hasidism's founding figures, the paradigmatic creation of Hasidism; that element of its overall historical record that alone stood before the modern West as spiritually compelling.

These considerations prepare us for the materials compiled in the present volume. Here, as in so much of Buber's Hasidica, the method of bringing the reader into communication with the essence of Hasidism is twofold. On the one hand, Buber selects and interpretatively renders Hasidic stories and epigrams which, in his judgment, bring the reader before the distinctive existential stance to which Hasidism as a whole points. Examples of this work appear in books III-V below.

On the other hand, Buber constructs interpretive essays, in which he formulates the mode of life revealed in the story into a body of propositions about redeemed human existence. These propositions—philosophical perspectives generated by reflection upon the tale—in turn become critical tools for illuminating the self-deceptions fostered by modern secularity. Book VI, in which Buber argues that modernity's separation of the religious dimension of life from the ethical and social has deprived the holy of its power to engage human consciousness, serves as a typical example.

Buber's strategy as a teacher of the Hasidic way, then, is to draw the reader, through the art of the tale, into an imaginative participation in the world of Hasidism at the moment of its creative genius. On the basis of that participation, he then draws out its implications by guiding the reader in the criticism of the modern world-view which, prior to confronting the Hasidic text, appeared self-evident and self-sufficient. The Hasidic text rendered by Buber, in other words, serves to shake the reader out of the familiar terms of his or her prior self-understanding. Thus estranged from a mode of life that fosters alienation from the world, the reader is in a position to find in Buber's interpretive essays concepts by which the reality of the Hasidic world may be appropriated, strategies for regenerating one's capacity to face the world and others as possibilities of liberation rather than obstacles to be manipulated and overcome.

The legitimate question to raise of Buber's work is whether in his renderings of Hasidic texts the reader in fact comes eye-to-eye (as Buber has put it above) with Hasidism. Is one not rather eye-to-eye with Buber? Perhaps, as Scholem already has argued, Buber's effectiveness as an interpreter of Hasidism has more to do with his literary gifts than with the intrinsic literary merits of the Hasidic tale or the truths to which they testify.

Buber, of course, must hold that however much

he has transformed Hasidic literature in helping it to engage the modern reader, his transformation has served rather than subverted the original intention of the Hasidic masters. As Buber tells us below, he has attempted to uncover "something that hid itself in Hasidism and would, or rather should, go out into the world" (22).[12] So Buber acknowledges that the legitimacy of his own literary project hinges to some admittedly vague degree upon an accurate depiction of Hasidism, regardless of whether or not the original Masters would have endorsed his own formulation of their teachings or his attempt to interpret them to a secular audience.

The historical question, therefore, appears critical: Is Buber right about Hasidism? If not, and if historians of religion can prove that he is not, what is the meaning of his work? Without wishing to defend Buber's presentation of Hasidism or to attack it, may I suggest that to a certain degree the historical question, while appropriate in its place, is also somewhat misdirected. The reader will recall that Buber's historical interest is in the re-presentation of creative moments of the human spirit, so that we, conditioned to uncritical acceptance of the assumptions of our own age, can be regenerated through them. Buber wants us to re-experience, with him, a past moment so that it can be made present and serve as the foundation for future decisions in our lives. This task is hardly that of the historian of religion, who, at most, is charged with making past moments *intelligible* to our understanding, so that, from our own perspective, we can appreciate creations of the human imagination which might be otherwise culturally inaccessible.

Buber's task and that of the historian of religion differ primarily in conceiving what is meant by historical understanding. For Buber, knowledge is genuinely historical if it obliterates the barrier of time and enables communication between the past and the contemporary knower. History is a category of experience by which vanished human lives are enabled to address us again through their texts. Historical understanding, therefore, is conceived on the model of communication between persons; we know the other, present or historically distant, through an act of interpretive self-opening that establishes a common world of relationship. In this act, history is overcome as an irretrievable distance, and the person of the past is made present as one's contemporary interlocutor. As in any personal encounter, the reader is changed by encountering the person speaking through the text, and the text itself—that is, its meaning—is enriched through its embodiment in the person of the reader, who brings the text into the world of his or her own experience.[13]

This conception of historical knowledge bears with it a certain ethic, if you will; an ethic analogous to that which obtains between two persons in a mutual encounter. One hears the other and one responds with one's whole person. One also respects the person and integrity of the other and refrains from reducing the other's self-opening to abstract, impersonal "factors" that deprive the other of his or her uniqueness. So too it is with the "other" who meets us in the text.

The moral burden of historical knowledge is to refrain from reducing the person who speaks in the text to an object, a sum of the social forces or causal sequences that issue in the creation of the text.[14]

The situation of interpretation is rather different for the historian of religion. Here the barrier of time that separates us from the past is not a hindrance to understanding but rather its very condition. Historical knowledge, if it is to constitute a form of knowledge unavailable to the participants in historical events (and thus be a source of genuine insight into the causes and motives of their actions), must preserve the distance of the knower from the known, just as, for example, the psychotherapist preserves distance from the analysand.

The reason is that the historian's task is not one of communion but of evaluation and discrimination; or skepticism and suspicion rather than of self-opening. In this view, historical texts, such as those produced within the Hasidic movement, are sufficiently understood only when their grounding in a reconstructed context of social and intellectual influences can be demonstrated. Hasidism is understood not by experiencing its uniqueness as presence but, rather, by placing it in perspective, by showing its relations to other things.

For this model of historical knowledge, the text of the past is much like the biologist's specimen. It is a dead thing that constitutes a kind of puzzle: Given such an organism, what constitutes the conditions which permit it to enter into the processes of life, to be born, to generate offspring, to mature and to die?

A text subject to such analysis remains as dead as the biologist's specimen. Neither the historian of religion nor the biologist claims (at least not yet) to bring the dead to life.

Clearly, the historian of religion's understanding of a particular moment in the history of a tradition such as Hasidism has little—in motive or result—to do with the kind of understanding sought by Martin Buber in his Hasidic writings. Whether the Hasidism to which he attempts to give new life is "really" Hasidism ceases to be at issue, for one might raise the same question of the Hasidism revealed under the analytical knife of the historian of religion.

"Historical" Hasidism, precisely because it is deprived by the historian of its power to make a moral claim upon the present, is hardly the reality that in its own day transformed the spritual lives of millions of Eastern European Jews and continues to shape the spirituality of a significant sector of contemporary Jewry. Buber's "interpretive" Hasidism, to the contrary, however much it might be a creation of the Buberian philosophy, does share with its historical forbear, at least in principle, the power to make a moral claim upon our attention. Its intention, no less than the vanished Hasidism of the Baal Shem Tov, is, after all, to shape life and to transform it. Whether one form of mis-truth is more desirable than the other, and whether Hasidism is best known dead or alive—these are questions that only the contemporary reader can answer. Certainly, the extent to which Buber's Hasidism enjoys a new life through the publication of this and other of his Hasidic studies will constitute part of that answer.

NOTES

1. The essays of both volumes, in the original German, have been collected in Martin Buber, *Werke. Dritter Band: Schriften Zum Chassidismus* (Munich and Heidelberg: Kösel-Verlag; 1963). The original publication dates and places of the essays are recorded on pp. 1269–70 of that volume.

2. "Judaism and Mankind," in *On Judaism* (New York: Schocken; 1972), p. 28.

3. Ibid., p. 29.

4. Ibid., pp. 30–31. Buber did not regard all periods of the history of Judaism as equally worthy of contemporary emulation. Indeed, he regarded the post-biblical religion of the rabbis as a frequently barren effort to capture an essentially free God in the institutional web of law and ritual. Rather, his interest lay in those moments in which great spirits transcended the institutional religiosity of their own day to retrieve a living experience of the source of religious life. Hence his admiration for Jesus, on the one hand, and medieval Jewish mystics, on the other. For Buber's critique of Rabbinic Judaism, see, for example, "The Renewal of Judaism", ibid., pp. 44–49, and "Myth in Judaism", ibid., pp. 98–100; for his general critique of religion as an attempt to reify an essentially free God, see *I and Thou*, trans. W. Kaufmann (New York: Scribners; 1970), pp. 160–68, and "Symbolic and Sacramental Existence," in *The Origin and Meaning of Hasidism* (New York: Harper Torchbook; 1960), pp. 168–69.

5. "The Spirit of the Orient and Judaism", in ibid., p. 75.

6. In this sense, the early Buber's "cultural Zionism," which sees the Jewish return to Zion as an historical event that testifies to processes occurring at a hidden level of spirit, shares much with the controversial visionary Abraham Isaac Kook, who saw in secular Zionism confirmation of certain elements of late-medieval Kabbalistic eschatology. For Kook's views, see the selections of his work anthologized in A. Hertzberg, *The Zionist Idea* (New York: Antheneum; 1977), pp. 417–31, and B. Z. Bokser, trans., *Abraham Isaac Kook: The Lights of Penitence, The Moral Principles, Lights of Holiness, Essays, Letters and Poems* (New York, Ramsey, Toronto: Paulist Press; 1978), pp. 126–28, 256–302.

7. "The Spirit of the Orient and Judaism," in *Origin and Meaning of Hasidism*, pp. 76–77.

8. See, for example, "Redemption," in *Origin and Meaning of Hasidism*, pp. 206–218.

9. See, for example, "The Holy Way: A Word to the Jews and the Nations," *On Judaism*, pp. 139–148.

10. "Redemption," in *Origin and Meaning of Hasidism*, p. 218.

11. See G. Scholem, "Martin Buber's Interpretation of Hasidism", *The Messianic Idea in Judaism* (New York: Schocken; 1971), pp. 227–50. More recently Scholem's critique has been (with less generosity than one might have wished) echoed and amplified by Steven T. Katz in "Buber's Misuse of Hasidic Sources," *Post-Holocaust Dialogues: Critical Studies in Modern Jewish Thought* (New York and London: New York University Press; 1983), pp. 52–93. A useful discussion of the issues of historical interpretation which inform the debate between Buber and Scholem on the nature of Hasidism may now be consulted in Steven D.

Kepnes, "A Hermeneutic Approach to the Buber-Scholem Controversy," *Journal of Jewish Studies*, 38:1 (Spring 1987): 81–98. For a perspective on this debate informed by recent trends in "deconstructive" literary criticism, see Laurence J. Silberstein, "Textualism, Literary Theory and the Modern Interpretation of Judaism," in M. L. Raphael, ed., *Approaches to Modern Judaism* (Chico: Scholars Press; 1984), I, pp. 6–8.

12. See Paul Mendes-Flohr's introduction to *The Tales of Rabbi Nachman* in the present series for a full discussion of Buber's method in bringing the message of the Hasidic tale to light.

13. See, for example Buber's discussion of the impact upon him of the tales of the Baal Shem Tov in "The Foundation Stone," in *Origin and Meaning of Hasidism*, p. 71: "Reality calls forth reality; the reality of a man who has lived in intercourse with the reality of being in its fullness, awakens the reality in us and helps us to live in intercourse with the reality of being in its fullness."

14. For further discussion of Buber's hermeneutics and its relationship to that of his teacher, Wilhelm Dilthey, see Kepnes, "A Hermeneutic Approach," pp. 82–87.

Martin S. Jaffee

EDITOR'S INTRODUCTION

Hasidism is the popular communal mysticism that went far toward transforming the face of East European Jewry in the eighteenth and nineteenth centuries. The Hasidic movement arose in Poland in the eighteenth century and, despite bitter persecution at the hands of traditional Rabbinism, spread rapidly among the Jews of eastern Europe until it included almost half of them in its ranks. The essays in this volume are concerned with the life of the Hasidim, as Martin Buber has expressed and interpreted it. Hasidism, as Buber portrays it, is a mysticism which hallows community and everyday life rather than withdraws from it, "for man cannot love God in truth without loving the world."

Martin Buber is the leading exponent of the "philosophy of dialogue"—a new and important view of human existence which has revolutionized much contemporary Jewish and Christian religious philosophy and whose no less decisive implications for psychology, education, ethics, and social thought are already beginning to be felt.* Along with his "I-Thou" philosophy and in fruitful interrelation with it, Buber is

* For a complete bibliography of Buber's works and a comprehensive study of his thought, see Maurice S. Friedman, *Martin Buber: The Life of Dialogue* (The University of Chicago Press, 1955).

best known for his re-creation of Hasidism. Buber's discovery of Hasidism was epochal for Western Jewry. He "made the thesis believable," writes Robert Weltsch, "that no renewal of Judaism would be possible which did not bear in itself elements of Hasidism." Through his Hasidic writings Buber has exerted significant influence on the Jewish movement and has initiated into the realm of Jewish culture many thousands of Jews devoid of Jewish background. By his almost single-handed labors, he has transformed Hasidism in the eyes of modern man from a little-known movement, misprized and neglected by the whole of Western culture, into one of the recognized great mystical movements of the world.*

In his earlier writings Buber regarded Hasidism as the real, though subterranean, Judaism as opposed to official rabbinism which was only the outer husk. He has since come to feel that in Hasidism the essence of Jewish faith and religiousness was visible in the structure of the community but that this essence has also been present "in a less condensed form everywhere in Judaism," in the "inaccessible structure of the personal life." Buber differs from other interpreters in regarding the life of the Hasidim as the core of Hasi-

* In the light of the importance in Buber's total work of his lifetime of Hasidic writings, it is incomprehensible to me that Will Herberg should not have included a single selection from them in his anthology *The Writings of Martin Buber*. This defect is happily and amply remedied in Jacob Trapp's forthcoming Martin Buber anthology *To Hallow This Life*.

dism and the philosophical texts as a gloss on the life as it is depicted in the legends. Not only his collections of Hasidic tales but even his interpretive essays, accordingly, start ever again from a legend, tale, or saying, and such works in the present volume as "The Life of the Hasidim," "The Way of Man," and "The Baal-Shem-Tov's Instruction" are largely built around the form, the interrelation, and the context that Buber has given to individual tales and sayings. Technical criticism of Buber's Hasidic legends is beside the point, writes Ludwig Lewisohn. They "will remain a permanent possession of mankind in the form he has given them by virtue of that form which has itself become a part of their message and meaning." It is to Buber's re-creation of Hasidism that Hermann Hesse pointed when he nominated Buber for a Nobel Prize in literature in 1949: "He has enriched world literature with a genuine treasure as has no other living author," wrote Hesse, "—the Tales of the Hasidim."*

The short works collected in *Hasidism and Modern Man* are remarkable at once for their variety of form and their unity of spirit. The title essay, the most recent of all (1957), serves as an introduction not only to this volume but also to the following one; for in this essay Martin Buber looks back over his half century of work in interpreting Hasidism and bringing it to the West and distills out of this variegated labor the simple, central message which he has more and

* See Martin Buber, *Tales of the Hasidim: The Early Masters* (1947), *The Later Masters* (1948), Shocken Books, New York.

more come to see as the core of Hasidic life and teaching: "Man cannot approach the divine by reaching beyond the human; he can approach Him through becoming human. To become human is what he, this individual man, has been created for."

The second selection, "My Way to Hasidism," was written almost forty years before (1918) and expresses certain attitudes toward the perfected man's realization of God in the world that differ substantially from Buber's later emphasis on the meeting and dialogue with God. In 1923, after the publication of *I and Thou,* the classic expression of his philosophy of dialogue, Buber wrote concerning his own earlier use of the concept of the "realization of God":

> It can . . . mislead one to the opinion that God is an "idea" which only through man becomes "reality" and further to the hopelessly perverted conception that God is not, but rather becomes—in man or in mankind. . . . Only through the primal certainty of divine being can we come into contact with the mysterious meaning of divine becoming.*

Despite this difference in emphasis, "My Way to Hasidism" is the perfect complement to "Hasidism and Modern Man" as an autobiographical introduction to Buber's own relation to Hasidism which helps us understand the essentially modern significance of the works that have come out of that relationship.

Book III of this volume, "The Life of the Hasidim,"

* Martin Buber, *Reden über das Judentum* ("Talks on Judaism," 1923), Foreword.

belongs to the earliest strata of Buber's interpretations of Hasidism. It was written in 1908 as the first section of Buber's second book, *The Legend of the Baal-Shem.* It is of this early material that Buber writes in "Hasidism and Modern Man":

> I did not yet know how to hold in check my inner inclination to transform poetically the narrative material. I did not, to be sure, bring in any alien motifs; still I did not listen attentively enough to the crude and ungainly, but living folk-tone which could be heard from this material.

As a result he stressed the purity and loftiness of Hasidism at the expense of its popular vitality. Buber distinguishes here, however, between the representation of Hasidic teaching, such as "The Life of the Hasidim," and the legends. The former was essentially faithful whereas the latter were modernized in the retelling. The poetic quality, the lofty spiritual tone, the aesthetic interweaving of quotation and narration—all set "The Life of the Hasidim" apart from the other works in this volume. Moreover, the emphasis on mystic ecstasy, even though accompanied by equal emphasis on service, intention, and humility, stands in contrast to Buber's later emphasis on the hallowing of the everyday as the essence of Hasidism. There is a suggestion here of mystic unity, of the perfection of the "loving man," of the self as a part of the all which stands in contrast with Buber's later philosophy of dialogue as well as his mature interpretation of Hasidism. Nonetheless, it is precisely here that one is compelled to recognize the remarkable unity of spirit that pervades the various stages and forms of Buber's Hasidic interpretation. Ecstasy is complemented by service, unity by duality; speech is the bearer of reality rather than the veil hiding it; and "the legend is the myth of I and Thou." "The Life of the Hasidim" is a remarkable poetic presentation of the full range of Hasidic life and teaching.

The fourth book, "The Way of Man according to the Teachings of Hasidism" (1948) is an entirely different kind of work from any of the others in this collection or, for that matter, any of Buber's other Hasidic writings. It consists of six sections, each in the form of a commentary on a Hasidic tale, supplemented by other tales and sayings. Yet it is far more than a mere interpretation or summary of Hasidic teaching. No other of Buber's works gives us so much of his own simple wisdom as this remarkable distillation. I should not hesitate to rank "The Way of Man" with *I and Thou* and Buber's Hasidic chronicle-novel *For the Sake of Heaven* as one of his great and enduring classics. One must not be concerned with individual salvation, Buber writes here: one begins with oneself, searching one's heart and finding one's particular way, but one must not be preoccupied with oneself but with "letting God into the world."

Book V, "The Baal-Shem-Tov's Instruction in Intercourse with God" (1928), belongs to the mature but not the latest period of Buber's interpretation of Hasidism. Here Buber's selection of quotations from the Baal-Shem on such aspects of the way as knowledge, fervor and work, distance and nearness, true intention, the might of words, distracting thoughts, pride and humility gives us our clearest single picture of the Baal-Shem, but unfiltered through the powerful transforming medium of Buber's thought and style, and it is instructive for this reason to compare some of these quotations with the occasionally poeticized versions that appear in "The Life of the Hasidim." Here one can see the great force and vitality of the Baal-Shem and can readily understand why it was the words of this man that brought the powerful conversion of which Buber tells in "My Way to Hasidism." Particularly startling to the modern reader, perhaps because we are so far from really believing with Hasidism that the profane is the not-yet-hallowed, are the Baal-Shem's forthright analogies between sexual intercourse and man's relation to God in prayer.

This book also reflects a second conversion, the one of which Buber tells in "Dialogue" in *Between Man and Man*. In his youth Buber was a mystic, given to hours of exaltation and rapture. Once after a morning of "religious enthusiasm," he was visited by a youth who came with an unstated question which he later learned was a matter of life and death. Though friendly and attentive, he was not, he says, really present in spirit. He did not meet the young man's despair by "a presence by means of which we are told that nevertheless there is a meaning." Buber regarded this event as a judgment and gave up the practice of a religious ecstasy which would take him out of everyday life. "Since then," he writes, "I know no fullness but each mortal hour's fullness of claim and responsibility." It took the first conversion to bring Buber to "The Life of the Hasidim," but it took the second, plus the realization that "The way is there that one may walk on it," to bring him to "The Baal-Shem-Tov's Instruction" and "The Way of Man." In the Foreword to "The Baal-Shem-Tov's Instruction" Buber points out that the Baal-Shem is the founder of a realist and active mysticism "for which the world is not an illusion from which man must turn away in order to reach true being." And in the highly important explanatory notes at the end of this book, he clarifies further the decisive step in the way that he has taken in coming to his philosophy of dialogue: the step from religion as man's "realization" of the divine in the world to religion as man's meeting with the "Eternal Thou," the "Absolute Person."

Man's power to reunite God with His Shekina—His exiled immanence—has its truth in the inwardness of the here and now, Buber writes here, but it in no way means a division of God, a unification which takes place in God, or any diminution of the fullness of His transcendence.

Book VI, "Love of God and Love of Neighbor" (1943), is the only selection in this volume that may be called an essay in the ordinary sense of the term. Unlike the others it is a systematic discussion of a problem: the relation of religion and ethics. But because it brings together Hasidism and modern thinking (particularly Kierkegaard) within the framework of this problem and because it focuses on the Hasidic understanding of love, it serves as an excellent commentary and conclusion to the other selections, into which this latter theme has been woven in so many ways. It is for this reason that this one essay from Buber's *Die chassidische Botschaft* ("The Message of Hasidism") appears in this volume.

Hasidism and Modern Man is the first of a two-volume collection of Martin Buber's interpretations of Hasidism, the second volume of which will appear as *The Origin and Meaning of Hasidism*, the two together to be called *Hasidism and The Way of Man*. The essays in the second volume explain the way in which Hasidism took over its central concepts from the Kabbala and transformed them from theosophy and gnosis into the way of man and the hallowing of the everyday. I have worked out the contents and order of these two volumes with the cooperation and approval of Professor Buber.

The translation of all the books in *Hasidism and Modern Man* is mine, with the exception of *The Way of Man*. We should like to acknowledge the kind permission of Routledge and Kegan Paul Ltd. to publish their translation of *The Way of Man according to the Teachings of the Hasidim* and of Harper and Brothers to reprint the section "The Life of the Hasidim" from Martin Buber, *The Legend of the Baal-Shem*, translated by Maurice Friedman (1955).

—MAURICE FRIEDMAN

Bronxville, New York
1958

BOOK I

HASIDISM AND MODERN MAN

It is more than fifty years since I began to acquaint the West with that religious movement known as Hasidism, which arose in the eighteenth century but extends into our time. If today, reporting and clarifying, I wish to speak of that work as a whole, this is not—I think I can say this with confidence—for the sake of my personal work. In performing this work I never had anything else in mind than an honest artisan has when he carries out a commission to the best of his ability. I speak, rather, for the sake of that to which my work wished and wishes to point. Much in it has at times been misunderstood and needs clarification.

Commission, I said—but is this comparison permissible? Was there someone who commissions? No, that there certainly was not; no one told me that he needed what I then made. And yet, it has also not been a literary project. There was something that commanded me, yes, which even took hold of me as an instrument at its disposal. What was that? Perhaps just Hasidism itself? It certainly was not this. Hasidism wishes to work exclusively within the boundaries of Jewish tradition and to concern no one outside of them. It was—so I might even venture to express it—something that hid itself in Hasidism and would, or rather should, go out into the world. To help it do this I was not unsuited.

Now I was still at that time, to be sure, an immature man; the so-called *Zeitgeist* still had power over me. To my readiness to make an adequate testimony to the great reality of faith disclosed to me through books and men was joined something of the widespread tendency of that time to display the contents of foreign religions to readers who wavered between desire for information and sheer curiosity. Besides, I did not yet know how to hold in check my inner inclination to transform poetically the narrative material. I did not, to be sure, bring in any alien motifs; still I did not listen attentively enough to the crude and ungainly but living folk-tone which could be heard from this material. At work in me here, too, was a natural reaction against the attitude of most Jewish historians of the nineteenth century toward Hasidism, in which they found nothing but wild superstition. The need, in the face of this misunderstanding, to point out the purity and loftiness of Hasidism led me to pay all too little attention to its popular vitality. Thus I can today to some extent still affirm these early attempts as a piece of work; as fulfillment of the task placed upon me, however, they have long since ceased to satisfy me. The representation of the Hasidic teaching that I gave in them was essentially faithful; but where I retold the legendary tradition, I still did so just as the Western author that I was.

Only in the course of the decade that followed the first publications did my authorship become a service, even though its independence could naturally only grow, and not lessen.

In the year before the first World War, the approach of the first stage of a catastrophe in the most exact sense of the term became evident to me. At that time, I gradually began to realize what later, after the end of the War, fulminated within me to certainty: that the human spirit is either bound to existence or, even though it be of the most astonishing caliber, it is nothing before the decisive judgment. Note well, this was no question of a philosophical conviction; it was not a question of what is usually described as existentialism. It was a question, rather, of the claim of existence itself, which had grown irresistible. The realization that at that time grew in me, that of human life as the possibility of a dialogue with being, was only the intellectual expression of just this certainty or just this claim.

At the same time, but in a special osmosis with it, my relationship to Hasidism was ever more basically transformed. To be sure, I knew from the beginning that Hasidism was not a teaching which was realized by its adherents in this or that measure, but a way of life, to which the teaching provided the indispensable commentary. But now it became overpoweringly clear that this life was involved in a mysterious manner in the task that had claimed me. I could not become a Hasid. It would have been an unpermissible masquerading had I taken on the Hasidic manner of life—I who had a wholly other relation to Jewish tradition, since I must distinguish in my innermost being between what is commanded me and what is not commanded me. It was necessary, rather, to take into my own existence as much as I actually could of what had been truly exemplified for me there, that is to say, of the realization of that dialogue with being whose possibility my thought had shown me. I say, to be sure, "task," and I say, "It needed to be done." But in truth there was never anything like an intention or a project—it happened only as it happened.

That is what I sought to indicate when in the spring of 1924 in the Foreword to one of my Hasidic books* I wrote: "Since I began my work on Hasidic literature, I have done this work for the sake of the teaching and the way. But at that time I believed that one might relate to them merely as an observer. Since then I have realized that the teaching is there that one may learn it and the way that one may walk on it. The deeper I realized this, so much the more this work, against which my life measured and ventured itself, became for me question, suffering, and also even consolation."

Out of these transformations the work has taken shape in the special form in which I have now for the most part retold the crude and shapeless traditional material. It is, in my opinion, a valid form of literature, which I call legendary anecdote. It has not developed out of literary presuppositions on the path of literary attempts, but out of the simple necessity to create a verbal expression adequate to an overpowering objective reality. It was the reality of the exemplary lives, of the lives

* Martin Buber, *Der Grosse Maggid und Seine Nachfolge* (Frankfurt; Rütten und Loening, 1924).

reported as exemplary, of a great series of leaders of Hasidic communities. They were not reported in connected biography, but just in a tremendous series of instances, limited events in which something was at times spoken, not seldom, however, only done, only lived. Yet even the dumb happening spoke—it told the exemplary. And, indeed, it did not tell it didactically; no "moral" was attached to the event, but it spoke, even as a life-event speaks, and if a saying was included, its effect too was like that of a life-event. But since the whole was handed down in crude formlessness, the new teller was obliged to reconstruct the pure event, nothing less but also nothing more. Thus grew the form of the legendary anecdote. They are called anecdotes because each one of them communicates an event complete in itself, and legendary because at the base of them lies the stammering of inspired witnesses who witnessed to what befell them, to what they comprehended as well as to what was incomprehensible to them; for the legitimately inspired has an honest memory that can nonetheless outstrip all imagination.

This form has enabled me to portray the Hasidic life in such a way that it becomes visible as at once reality and teaching. Even where I had to let theory speak, I could relate it back to the life.

But I became more and more aware of a fact that has become of utmost significance to me: that the kernel of this life is capable of working on men even today, when most of the powers of the Hasidic community itself have been given over to decay or destruction, and it is just on the present-day West that it is capable of working in an especial manner. After the rise and decline of that life in the Polish, Ukrainian, Lithuanian ghettos, this kernel has entered into a contemporaneity, which is still, to be sure, only reminiscent, only an indication in the spirit, but even so can accomplish something in this manifestation that was basically foreign to the reality of that time. From here comes an answer to the crisis of Western man that has become fully manifest in our age. It is a partial answer only, not an ideological one, however, but one stemming directly out of reality and permeated by it. That life arose once as the reply of the primal Jewish faith to the utterly unfruitful exaltation of the pseudo-messianic movements of the seventeenth and eighteenth centuries which confounded redemption and liberation, even as they confounded the divine and the human. It opposed to this salvational confusion a hallowing of the everyday in which the demonic was overcome through being transformed.

II

What is of greatest importance in Hasidism, today as then, is the powerful tendency, preserved in personal as well as in communal existence, to overcome the fundamental separation between the sacred and the profane.

This separation has formed a part of the foundations of every religion. Everywhere the sacred is removed and set apart from the fullness of the things, properties, and actions belonging to the universal, and the sacred now forms in its totality a self-contained holiness outside of which the diffused profane must pitch its tent.

The consequence of this separation in the history of man is a twofold one. Religion is thereby assured a firm province whose untouchableness is ever again guaranteed it by the representatives of the state and of society, not, for the most part, without compensation. But at the same time the adherents of religion are thereby enabled to allow the essential application of their relation of faith to fulfill itself within this province alone without the sacred being given a corresponding power in the rest of life, and particularly in its public sphere.

In Judaism the border between the two realms appears at first glance to be drawn with utmost sharpness. To one coming from the outside, the great mass of rituals appears like something existing for itself. Moreover, even from within much testifies to the sharpness of this separation: thus the invocation of God spoken at the end of the Sabbath as that which separates the sacred from the profane. One need only note how many everyday actions are introduced by a blessing, however, to recognize how deep the hallowing reaches here into what is in itself unsanctified. One not only blesses God every morning on awakening because he has allowed one to awaken, but also when one begins to use a new house or piece of clothing or tool because one has been preserved in life to this hour. Thus the simple fact of continued earthly existence is here sanctified at each occasion that offers itself and thereby also this occasion itself. The concept is progressively formed, however, that the separation between the realms is only a provisional one. The commands of the religious law, accordingly, only delimit the sphere which is already claimed for hallowing, the sphere in which the preparation and education for every action's becoming holy takes place. In the messianic world all shall be holy. In Hasidism this tendency reaches a highly realistic consummation. The profane is now regarded only as a preliminary stage of the holy; it is the not-yet-hallowed. But human life is destined to be hallowed

How can anything created by God not be Holy - Are the creations of God profane? & if so is God or Aspects of God profane or unholy? If all is God & God is sacred then how can something be both sacred & profane unless God is himself?

in all its natural, that is, its created structure. "God dwells where one lets Him in," says a Hasidic saying; the hallowing of man means this letting in. Basically the holy in our world is nothing other than what is open to transcendence, as the profane is nothing other than what at first is closed off from it, and hallowing is the event of opening out.

Here a misunderstanding must be avoided. One readily ascribes to Judaism a "religious activism" which does not know the reality of grace and pursues vain self-hallowing or self-salvation. In reality, in Judaism the relation between man's action and God's grace is guarded as a mystery, even as that between human freedom and God's all-knowing, a mystery which is ultimately identical with that of the relation between God and man. Man cannot take himself in hand, so to speak, in order to hallow himself: he is never in his own hand. But there is something that he has retained as a creature, something that is given over just to him and expected just from him; it is called the beginning. A saying explains the opening word of the Hebrew Bible, the word *b'reshit,* "In the beginning," in this fashion: the world was created for the sake of the beginning, for the sake of making a beginning, for the sake of the human beginning-ever-anew. The fact of creation means an ever renewed situation of choice. Hallowing is an event which commences in the depths of man, there where choosing, deciding, beginning takes place. The man who thus begins enters into the hallowing. But he can only do this if he begins just as man and presumes to no superhuman holiness. The true hallowing of a man is the hallowing of the human in him. Therefore the Biblical command, "Holy men shall you be unto me" has received Hasidic interpretation thus: "*Humanly* holy shall you be unto me."

In life, as Hasidism understands and proclaims it, there is, accordingly, no essential distinction between sacred and profane spaces, between sacred and profane times, between sacred and profane actions, between sacred and profane conversations. At each place, in each hour, in each act, in each speech the holy can blossom forth. As an example that rises to symbolic heights, I cite the story of Rabbi Shmelke's sleep. In order that his study in the holy books should not suffer too long interruption, Rabbi Shmelke used to sleep in no other way than sitting, his head on his arm; but between his fingers he held a burning candle that awakened him as soon as the flame touched his hand. When Rabbi Elimelech visited him and recognized the still imprisoned might of his holiness, he carefully prepared for him a couch and induced him with much persuasion to stretch himself out on it for a while. Then he shut and darkened the window. Rabbi Shmelke only awoke when it was already broad daylight. He noticed how long he had slept, but it did not bother him; for he felt an unknown, sun-like clarity. He went into the prayer house and prayed before the community, as was his custom. To the community, however, it appeared as if they had never before heard him, so did the might of his holiness compel and liberate all. When he sang the song of the Red Sea, they had to pull up their caftans in order that the waves rearing up to the right and the left should not wet them.

Here the anti-ascetic character of Hasidic teaching also finds expression. No mortification of the urges is needed, for all natural life can be hallowed: one can live it with holy intention. The Hasidic teaching likes to explain this intention in connection with the kabbalistic myth of the holy sparks. With the "breaking of the world-vessels," which in the era before creation could not withstand the creative overflow, sparks have fallen into all things and are now imprisoned in them until ever again a man uses a thing in holiness and thus liberates the sparks that it conceals. "All that man possesses," says the founder of Hasidism, the Baal-Shem, "conceals sparks which belong to the root of his soul and wish to be elevated by him to their origin." And he says further, "Therefore one should have mercy on his tools and all his possessions; one should have mercy on the holy sparks." Even in food there dwell holy sparks, and eating can be holier than fasting; the latter is only the preparation for hallowing, the former can be hallowing itself.

What Hasidism here expresses mythically is a central knowledge that is communicable only in images, not in concepts. But it is by no means exclusively bound to this one mythical tradition. The same teaching is expressed in a wholly different, Biblically-based image: "Every creature, plant and animal offers itself to man, but by man all is offered to God. When man with all his limbs purifies and hallows himself to an offering, he purifies and hallows the creature." Here the concept becomes still clearer that man is commissioned and summoned as a cosmic mediator to awaken a holy reality in things through holy contact with them.

The same basic thought attains expression, not in such traditional form but in a wholly personal way, in the conversation which has been preserved for us of a great *zaddik* with his son. He asks the son, "With what do you pray?" The son understands the meaning of the question to be, On what meditation do you base your prayer? He replies, "Everything of great stature shall bow before Thee." Then he asks the father, "And with what do you pray?" "With the floor," answers the father, "and with the bench." This is no metaphor; the word "with" is now meant quite directly: in praying the rabbi joins himself to the floor on which he stands and the bench on which he sits—they, the things that are, to be sure, made by human hand, yet like all things have their origin in God, help him to pray. And he helps them pray, indeed; he raises them, the wooden floor and the wooden bench, to origin, to their origin, he "elevates" them.

But this "elevation" is by no means to be understood as removing the worldly character of things or spiritualizing the world, although something of this is to be found in Hasidic doctrine. The life of which I speak, the exemplary life, has proved itself stronger than the thought, and in the measure that the teaching became the commentary of this life, it had to adapt itself to it. What is ultimately in question here finds naive yet true expression in another narrative. It is told of a zaddik that one once spoke before him of the great misery of the human race. Sunk in grief, he listened. Then he raised his head. "Let us," he cried, "draw God into the world, and all will be stilled." One must not understand this bold speech as if a presumptuous "activism" comes to words in it. It stems rather from the same spirit as that saying which we have already quoted, "God dwells where one lets Him in." God wants—that is the meaning of it—to dwell in the world, but only when the world wants to let Him in. Let us, the Hasidic rabbi says to the world, prepare for God a dwelling-place into which He desires to enter; when it is prepared by us, by the world of its own will—we let God in. The hallowing of the world will be this letting-in. But grace wants to help the world to hallow itself.

None of this presupposes, however, that God does not dwell in His creation. That would indeed contradict that verse of the Scriptures in which it is said of God, He makes His dwelling "with them in the midst of their uncleanness," a verse which does not speak, to be sure, of a permanent dwelling—that would be described otherwise—but just of a temporary residing. Also the post-Biblical conception of the Shekina, later given manifold mythical development by the mystics and intimately familiar to Hasidism, the conception of the divine "indwelling," a hypostasis or emanation that joins itself to the human race exiled from Paradise, or to Israel driven out of its land, and wanders with it over the earth—it too means only the divine participation in the destiny of His sinful and suffering creation: the work of the "stilling" of this suffering, of which the Hasidic tale speaks, is no longer of a historical nature. Here, as ever again in Hasidism, the eschatological conception breaks into the lived hour and permeates it.

We must, therefore, distinguish within Hasidic life and Hasidic teaching between two kinds of "letting God in." This distinction can be clarified through looking once more at two different sayings.

The one is attached to the conception of the Shekina. The verse of the Psalm, "A stranger am I on the earth, do not conceal from me your commandment," was expounded thus by a zaddik: "You are, like me, a stranger on the earth and your indwelling has no resting place: So do not withdraw yourself from me, but disclose to me your commandment so that I can become your friend." God helps with His nearness the man who wants to hallow himself and his world.

In order to understand correctly what manner of existence is meant here, we will do well to place another saying of the same zaddik by its side: "The sparks which fell down from the primal creation into the covering shells and were transformed into stones, plants, and animals, they all ascend to their source through the consecration of the pious who works on them in holiness, uses them in holiness, consumes them in holiness." Thus is the man created who calls himself a stranger on earth.

The second saying stems from a later zaddik. It runs, "The peoples of the earth also believe that there are two worlds; 'in that world,' they say. The difference is this: they understand the two worlds to be removed and cut off from each other. But Israel believes that the two worlds are one in their ground and that they shall become one in their reality."

Only the two sayings taken together give us the basic content of Hasidic faith.

III

The central example of the Hasidic overcoming of the distance between the sacred and the profane points to an explanation of what is to be understood by the fact that Hasidism has its word to speak in the crisis of Western man.

This crisis was already recognized by Kierkegaard a hundred years ago as an unprecedented shaking of the foundations of man as man. But it is only in our generation that we have seriously begun to occupy ourselves with the fact that in this crisis something begins to be decided that is bound up in the closest manner with a decision about ourselves.

Modern thinkers have undertaken to give a causal explanation of the crisis through various partial aspects: Marx through the radical "alienation" of man caused by the economic and technical revolutions, and the psychoanalysts through individual or even collective neuroses. But no one of these attempts at explanation nor all of them together can yield an adequate understanding of what concerns us. We must take the injured wholeness of man upon us as a life burden in order to press beyond all that is merely symptomatic, and grasp the true sickness through which those motifs receive the force to work as they have worked. Those who, instead of this, contemplate the cruel problematic as a subject of unsurpassable interest, who know how to describe and even perhaps to praise it, contribute, at times with the highest gifts, to the massive decisionlessness whose true name is the decision for nothing.

An especially threatening trait of the crisis is the secularized form of the radical separation between the sacred and the profane. The sacred has become in many cases a concept empty of reality, now of merely historical and ethnological significance. But its character of detachment has found an heir. One no longer knows the holy face to face; but one believes that one knows and cherishes its heir, the "spiritual," without, of course, allowing it the right to determine life in any way. The spirit is hedged in and its claim on personal existence is warded off through a comprehensive apparatus; one can now enjoy it without having to fear awkward consequences. One has ideas, one just has them and displays them to one's own satisfaction and occasionally also to that of others. One seems to take them with grim seriousness; but that must be the end of it. One enthrones them on golden thrones to which their limbs are chained. No false piety has ever attained this concentrated degree of inauthenticity.

Only now has one basically got rid of the holy and the command of hallowing.

Over against all this behavior of present-day man, Hasidism sets the simple truth that the wretchedness of our world is grounded in its resistance to the entrance of the holy into lived life. The spirit was not spun in the brain; it has been from all eternity, and life can receive it into human reality. A life that does not seek to realize what the living person, in the ground of his self-awareness, understands or glimpses as the right is not merely unworthy of the spirit; it is also unworthy of life.

Especially important within the secularized division between the above and the below is the sickening of our contact with things and beings. The thinking of the age knows how to speak about things and beings in an illuminating fashion, but the great insight that our relations to things and beings form the marrow of our existence seems to have become alien to life. The Hasidic teaching of the holy intercourse with all existing beings opposes this corrosion of the living power of meeting as the progressive evasion of man before the meeting with God in the world.

IV

I have not converted the message of Hasidism into solid concepts; I was concerned to preserve its mythical as well as its epic essence. I cannot concur with the postulate of the hour—to demythologize religion. For myth is not the subsequent clothing of a truth of faith; it is the unarbitrary testimony of the image-making vision and the image-making memory, and the conceptual cannot be refined out of it. No sermonic teaching can replace the myth; but there can certainly be sermonic teachings that are able to renew it through bearing it uninjured into the present. In order that this may be possible, where myth has taken on a gnostic nature, i.e., where it has been employed to represent the mystery of transcendent being as knowable, it must, of course, be freed from this nature, this unnatural state, and restored to its original condition. Such restoration and renewal was accomplished by Hasidism with the myths permeated by gnosis that it took over from the Kabbala. My transmitting of the Hasidic message is no speculative theology; where myth is here perceivable, it is one that has entered into the lived life of seven generations, as whose late-born interpreter I function.

In this form I have sought, in a lifelong work, to introduce the Hasidic life-teaching to present-day

Western man. It has often been suggested to me that I should liberate this teaching from its "confessional limitations," as people like to put it, and proclaim it as an unfettered teaching of mankind. Taking such a "universal" path would have been for me pure arbitrariness. In order to speak to the world what I have heard, I am not bound to step into the street. I may remain standing in the door of my ancestral house: here too the word that it uttered does not go astray.

The Hasidic word says that the worlds can fulfill their destiny of becoming one through man's life becoming one. But how can that be understood? Is then a completed unity of living thinkable anywhere else than in the transcendence itself? Israel's confession of the oneness of God says, indeed, not merely that outside of Him there is no God, but also that He alone is unity. Here the interpreter must enter in. If man can become "humanly holy," i.e., become holy as man, in the measure and in the manner of man, and, indeed, as it is written, "to Me," i.e., in the face of God, then he, the individual man, can also—in the measure of his personal ability and in the manner of his personal possibility—become one in the sight of God. Man cannot approach the divine by reaching beyond the human; he can approach Him through becoming human. To become human is what he, this individual man, has been created for. This, so it seems to me, is the eternal core of Hasidic life and of Hasidic teaching.

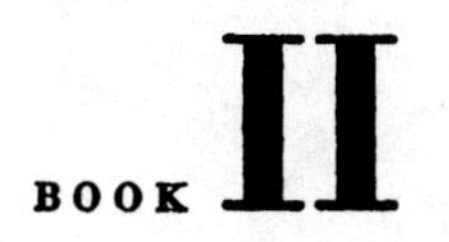

MY WAY TO HASIDISM

The Hebrew word "Hasid" means a pious man. There have again and again been communities in post-exilic Judaism that bore the name Hasidim, the pious: from those about which the first Book of Maccabees reports—a band remaining faithful to the teaching and fighting for it, and those, of whom the Mishna declares, "He who says, What is mine is thine, and what is thine is mine," i.e., he who claims for himself no possessions, "is a Hasid," up to those "Hasidim" whose other half thousand in the year 1700 journeyed under continual chastisements to the Holy Land in order to bring forth the messianic kingdom, and there perished. Finally there arose the community founded by Israel ben Eliezer, the Baal-Shem, around the middle of the eighteenth century, which fell into decay after a short period of flowering rich in memorable forms, but today* still embraces a large part of Eastern Jewry. What is common to all of them is that they wanted to take seriously their piety, their relation to the divine in earthly life; that they did not content themselves with the preaching of divine teaching and the practice of divine rituals, but sought to erect men's life-together on the foundation of divine truth. This is especially clear in the last-named community, with which I am here concerned.

The Jewish historian Graetz, partially under the influence of the views of the Jewish Enlightenment, cannot say anything of this "New Hasidism" other than that it is "wildest superstition." But a contemporary and friend of Graetz, Moses Hess, the founder of modern Zionism, made the deeply understanding statement that Hasidism forms within the living Jewish spirit the transition "from medieval Judaism to a regenerated Judaism which is only in formation"; its consequences are "incalculable when the national movement takes possession of it."

In fact, nowhere in the last centuries has the soul-force of Judaism so manifested itself as in Hasidism. The old power lives in it that once held the

* 1918—Ed.

immortal fast to earth, as Jacob the angel, in order that it might fulfill itself in mortal life. But at the same time a new freedom announces itself therein. Without an iota being altered in the law, in the ritual, in the traditional life-norms, the long-accustomed arose in a fresh light and meaning. Still bound to the medieval in its outward appearance, Hasidic Judaism is already open to regeneration in its inner truth, and the degeneration of this great religious movement can only halt but not stop entirely the process in the history of the spirit that began with it.

This is not the place to present the teachings of Hasidism. They can be summed up in a single sentence: God can be beheld in each thing and reached through each pure deed. But this insight is by no means to be equated with a pantheistic world view, as some have thought. In the Hasidic teaching, the whole world is only a word out of the mouth of God. Nonetheless, the least thing in the world is worthy that through it God should reveal Himself to the man who truly seeks Him; for no thing can exist without a divine spark, and each person can uncover and redeem this spark at each time and through each action, even the most ordinary, if only he performs it in purity, wholly directed to God and concentrated in Him. Therefore, it will not do to serve God only in isolated hours and with set words and gestures. One must serve God with one's whole life, with the whole of the everyday, with the whole of reality. The salvation of man does not lie in his holding himself far removed from the worldly, but in consecrating it to holy, to divine meaning: his work and his food, his rest and his wandering, the structure of the family and the structure of society. It lies in his preserving the great love of God for all creatures, yes, for all things. Hasidism took the social form of a great popular community—not an order of the secluded, not a brotherhood of the select, but a popular community in all its medley, in all its spiritual and social multiplicity. Never yet in Europe has such a community thus established the whole of life as a unity on the basis of the inwardly known. Here is no separation between faith and work, between truth and verification, or, in the language of today, between morality and politics; here all is one kingdom, one spirit, one reality.

In my childhood (at a very early age I came from Vienna, where I was born, to Galicia and grew up there with my grandparents) I spent every summer on an estate in Bukovina. There my father took me with him at times to the nearby village of Sadagora. Sadagora is the seat of a dynasty of "zaddikim" (*zaddik* means righteous, proven, completed), that is, of Hasidic rabbis. The "cultured" speak of "wonder rabbis" and believe they know about them. But, as is usual with the "cultured" in such matters, they possess only the most superficial information. The legendary greatness of the grandfathers has certainly disappeared in the grandsons and many are at pains to preserve their power through all kinds of petty magic; but all their carryings on cannot darken the inborn shining of their foreheads, cannot destroy the inborn sublimity of their figure: their unarbitrary nobility speaks more compellingly than all their arbitrariness. And certainly there no longer lives in the present-day community that high faith of the first hasidim, that fervent devotion which honored in the zaddik the perfected man in whom the immortal finds its mortal fulfillment. Rather the present-day hasidim turn to the zaddik above all as the mediator through whose intercession they hope to attain the satisfaction of their needs. But far removed from their lower wills, a shudder of profoundest reverence seizes them ever again when the *rebbe* stands in silent prayer or interprets the mystery of the Torah in hesitating speech at the third Sabbath meal. Even in these degenerate Hasidim there still continues to glow, in the unknown ground of their souls, the word of Rabbi Eliezar that the world was created for the sake of the perfected man (the zaddik), even though there should be only one; "for it says, 'And God saw the light, that it was good'; but 'good' means nothing other than the perfected man" (Talmud Babli, Yoma 38b).

This I realized at that time, as a child, in the dirty village of Sadagora from the "dark" Hasidic crowd that I watched—as a child realizes such things, not as thought, but as image and feeling—that the world needs the perfected man and that the perfected man is none other than the true helper. Certainly, the zaddik is now essentially approached for help in quite earthly needs. But is he not still what he once was imagined and appointed to be: the helper in spirit, the teacher of world-meaning, the conveyor to the divine sparks? Certainly, the power entrusted to him has been misinterpreted by the faithful, has been misused by himself. But is it not at base a legitimate, *the* legitimate power, this power of the helping soul over the needy? Does there not lie in it the seed of future social orders?

At any rate, in a childish fashion, these questions already dawned on me at that time. And I could compare: on the one side with the head man of the province whose power rested on nothing but habitual compulsion; on the other with the rabbi, who was an honest and God-fearing man, but an employee of the "directorship of the cult." Here, however, was another, an incomparable; here was, debased yet uninjured, the living double kernel of humanity: genuine *community* and genuine *leadership*. Ancient past, farthest future were here, lost, longed for, returned.

The palace of the rebbe, in its showy splendor, repelled me. The prayer house of the Hasidim with its enraptured worshippers seemed strange to me. But when I saw the rebbe striding through the rows of the waiting, I felt, "leader," and when I saw the hasidim dance with the Torah, I felt, "community." At that time there rose in me a presentiment of the fact that common reverence and common joy of soul are the foundations of genuine human community.

In boyhood this early presentiment began to slip away from me into the unconscious. I now spent the summers in another province and was finally close to forgetting the Hasidic impressions of my childhood. Then I came after many years to a newly-inherited estate of my father, in the neighborhood of Czortkov, a village which is the place of residence of a collateral line of the same dynasty of zaddikim. As there still lives in Sadagora the memory, handed down by generations, of the great "Rishiner" (so called because he had to flee out of Ruzyn in Berditschev, under suspicion by the Russian government as "King of the Jews," and after many wanderings settled in Sadagora), so in Czortkov there still lives today the direct recollection of his son David Moshe. Unfortunately I received nothing from him at that time. In any case, my impressions this time were paler and more fleeting. That might be caused by the fact that meanwhile I had been seized by the fermenting intellectuality which is often characteristic of the decisive years of youth and which puts an end to the natural seeing and experiencing of the child. Through this intellectuality I had become alienated from the hasidim; it robbed me of my naive affinity with their being. By virtue of my thinking I seemed to myself far removed from their world; indeed, I confess that I regarded Hasidism not essentially otherwise than Graetz does: I looked down on it from the heights of a rational man. I now saw nothing more of its life, even when I passed quite close to it—because I did not want to see anything.

In spite of this, at that period I heard for the first time, without paying any attention to it, the name that would mean the most precious discovery for me many years later: the name "Besht." This name is composed of the initial letters of the three words *Baal Shem Tov* (Master of the Good Name) and designates the founder of Hasidism, Rabbi Israel ben Eliezer (1700-1760). One of the dairy farms of that estate of my father's was called Tluste Village. In Tluste-City, the market town belonging to it (later well known through the reports from the front of the Russian supreme command, since it was fought over for a long time), the Baal-Shem had lived as a poor teacher of small children. Here, according to the report of the legend, a dream announced to him in the night when he had completed his thirty-third year that the time had come for him to go forth to men.

But it was not Hasidism alone from which I was alienated at that time, but Judaism as a whole.

I had spent my childhood, the time up to my fourteenth year, in the house of my grandfather, the Midrash scholar. The Midrash was the world in which Salomon Buber lived, lived with a wonderful concentration of soul, with a wonderful intensity of work. He edited text after text of the Midrash, those books of Bible interpretation, comparable to no other literature, abounding in legends, sayings, and noble parables. In the Midrash, scattered in a thousand fragments, is concealed a second Bible, the Bible of the exile. Without having ever appropriated the philological methods of the West, he revised the manuscripts with the reliability of the modern scholar and at the same time with the presence of knowledge of the Talmudic master who has directly at hand for each sentence and each word whatever relates to it in the entire literature—not as material of memory alone, but as an organic possession of the whole person. The spiritual passion which manifested itself in his incessant work was combined with the untouchable, inperturbable childlikeness of a pure human nature and an elementary Jewish being. When he spoke Hebrew (as he frequently did when foreign guests visited him from distant lands), it sounded like the speech of a prince returned home from exile. He did not trouble himself about Judaism, but it dwelled in him.

So long as I lived with him, my roots were firm, although many questions and doubts also jogged about in me. Soon after I left his house, the whirl of the age took me in. Until my twentieth year, and in small measure even beyond then, my spirit was in steady and multiple movement, in an alternation of tension and release, determined by manifold influences, taking ever new shape, but without center and without growing substance: it was really the *"Olam-ha-Tohu,"* the "World of Confusion," the mythical dwelling place of the wandering souls. Here I lived—in versatile fullness of spirit, but without Judaism, without humanity, and without the presence of the divine.

The first impetus toward my liberation came from Zionism. I can here only intimate what it meant for me: the restoration of the connection, the renewed taking root in the community. No one needs the saving connection with a people so much as the youth who is seized by spiritual seeking, carried off into the upper atmosphere by the intellect; but among the youths of this kind and this destiny none so much as the Jewish. The other peoples preserve from dissolution the deep inborn binding to the native soil and popular tradition inherited from millennia. The Jew, even with a feeling for nature acquired since yesterday and a cultivated understanding of, say, German popular art and customs, is directly threatened by such dissolution and abandoned to it so far as he does not find himself at home in his community. And the most sparkling wealth of intellectuality, the most luxuriant seeming productivity (only he who is bound can be genuinely productive) cannot compensate the detached man for the holy insignia of humanity—rootedness, binding, wholeness.

That Zionism seized me and that I was newly vowed to Judaism was, I repeat, only the first step. The acknowledgment of the nation does not by itself transform the Jewish man; he can be just as poor in soul with it as without it, even if, of course, not so rootless as without it. But to him to whom it is not a satiating but a soaring, not an entering into the harbor but a setting out on to the open sea—to him it can indeed lead to transformation. Thus it happened to me.

I professed Judaism before I really knew it. So this became, after some blind groping, my second step: wanting to know it. To know—by this I do not mean a storing up of anthropological, historical, sociological knowledge, as important as these are; I mean the immediate knowing, the eye-to-eye knowing of the people in its creative primal hours.

On this way I came to Hasidism.

In the world of confusion I had neglected my Hebrew, which had been very dear to me as a boy. Now I acquired it anew. I began to comprehend it in its essence, that cannot be adequately translated into any other, at least into any Western language. And I read—read, at first ever again repelled by the brittle, ungainly, unshapely material, gradually overcoming the strangeness, discovering the characteristic, beholding the essential with growing devotion. Until one day I opened a little book entitled the *Zevaat Ribesh*—that is the testament of Rabbi Israel Baal-Shem—and the words flashed toward me, "He takes unto himself the quality of fervor. He arises from sleep with fervor, for he is hallowed and become another man and is worthy to create and is become like the Holy One, blessed be He, when He created His world." It was then that, overpowered in an instant, I experienced the Hasidic soul. The primally Jewish opened to me, flowering to newly conscious expression in the darkness of exile: man's being created in the image of God I grasped as deed, as becoming, as task. And this primally Jewish reality was a primal human reality, the content of human religiousness. Judaism as religiousness, as "piety," as *Hasidut* opened to me there. The image out of my childhood, the memory of the zaddik and his community, rose upward and illuminated me: I recognized the idea of the perfected man. At the same time I became aware of the summons to proclaim it to the world.

But first came the time of study. At twenty-six, I withdrew myself for five years from activity in the Zionist party, from writing articles and giving speeches, and retired into the stillness; I gathered, not without difficulty, the scattered, partly missing, literature, and I immersed myself in it, discovering mysterious land after mysterious land.

My first communication, my "authorship," came about in a remarkable manner. Among all the books, the collections of oral teachings of the zaddikim and the collections of legends from their lives, there was one that was wholly distinctive, wholly separate from the others, and at the same time probably the most popular of all: the "Ssippure Massiyot," "Tales of Adventure," the stories of Rabbi Nachman of Bratzlav, a great-grandson of the Baal-Shem. These stories were told by Rabbi Nachman to his disciples, and after his death one of them wrote them down and published them in an obviously distorted form. These were in part pure fairy tales, in imitation, especially, of the Oriental, in other part creations of a special kind—symbolic, at times freely allegorizing tales. Common to all of them was a not actually didactic but certainly teaching trait; Rabbi Nachman himself had called them the clothes of his teachings, and a comprehensive commentary upon them had arisen from the hands of his disciples. But in them all there also remained the distortion—the distortion of the contents through all kinds of utilitarian and vulgar-rationalistic insertions, of the form through the confusion of lines and the muddying of the pure colors. This one can infer from a few striking parts.

Almost involuntarily I began to translate two of the real fairy tales, hence the unoriginal pieces of the book; if I thought of readers in so doing, then they were none other than children. When I had finished, what lay before me seemed to me paltrier than I had supposed, definitely inferior in quality to the related stories from the Thousand and One Nights. When I saw one of them printed,* I was altogether disappointed. It could not work out thus: in the reproduction in a foreign language the distortion was still more visible, the original form still more obscured. I noted that the purity did not allow itself to be preserved in translation, much less enhanced—I had to tell the stories that I had taken into myself from out of myself, as a true painter takes into himself the lines of the models and achieves the genuine images out of the memory

* In a collection for children, *Heim der Jugend*, with pictures by Hermann Struck; these tales were not included in my book *Die Geschichten des Rabbi Nachman* (1907), reprinted by Fischer Bücherei, 1955.

formed of them. I began, still shy and awkward, with "The Steer and the Ram." Becoming freer and surer, I turned to "The Simple Man and the Clever Man," then to "The King's Son and the Son of the Maid." "The Rabbi and His Son" was the first which grew unexpectedly into my own work. In the two last, "The Master of Prayer" and "The Seven Beggars,"* I experienced, even in the entirely new pieces that I inserted, my unity with the spirit of Rabbi Nachman. I had found the true faithfulness: more adequately than the direct disciples, I received and completed the task, a later messenger in a foreign realm.

I realized my inborn binding with Hasidic truth still more forcefully in the second book, *The Legend of the Baal-Shem,*** which sought to construct the inner process in the life of the master out of a selection of traditional legendary motifs which I took from folk books, later also from the mouth of the people themselves. Here too I had begun to

* These stories are all included in Martin Buber, *The Tales of Rabbi Nachman,* translated by Maurice Friedman (New York: The Horizon Press, 1956).

** *Die Legende des Baalschem* (1908), reprinted as a volume of the Manesse Bibliothek der Welt-Literature (1955), published in America and England as *The Legend of the Baal-Shem,* translated by Maurice Friedman (New York: Harper & Brothers, 1955; London: East and West Library, 1956).

translate, a short time after setting down the first tales of Rabbi Nachman. Here too I met with disappointment. The already-existing stories were for the most part recorded in crude and clumsy fashion; they did not become more winged in translation.* Thus here too I came to my own narrating in growing independence; but the greater the independence became, so much the more deeply I experienced the faithfulness. And therefore, although by far the largest part of the book is autonomous fiction composed from traditional motifs, I might honestly report of my experience of the legend: "I bore in me the blood and the spirit of those who created it, and out of my blood and spirit it has become new."

Since then, several years after the completion of both books, I discovered another manner of artistic faithfulness to the popular Hasidic narrative. But this no longer belongs to the context of this communication, the subject of which is my way to Hasidism.

But there undoubtedly belongs in this context a humorous and meaningful occurrence which took

* One of these translations (although already somewhat free), "Der Zukunftsbrief," appeared in the weekly *Die Welt,* but was not included in the book.

place in 1910 or 1911, and again, in fact, in Bukovina, not far from Sadagora, in Czernovitz, the capital of the country. After a lecture that I had delivered (it was the third of my *Three Talks on Judaism*), I went with some members of the association, who had arranged the evening into a coffee house. I like to follow the speech before many, whose form allows no reply, with a conversation with a few in which person acts on person and my view is set forth directly through going into objection and question.

We were just discussing a theme of moral philosophy when a well-built Jew of simple appearance and middle age came up to the table and greeted me. To my no doubt somewhat distant return greeting, he replied with words not lacking a slight reproof: "Doctor! Do you not recognize me?" When I had to answer in the negative, he introduced himself as M., the brother of a former steward of my father's. I invited him to sit with us, inquired about his circumstances of life and then took up again the conversation with the young people. M. listened to the discussion, which had just taken a turn toward somewhat abstract formulations, with eager attentiveness. It was obvious that he did not understand a single word; the devotion with which he received every word resembled that of the believers who do not need to know the content of a litany since the arrangement of sounds and tones alone give them all that they need, and more than any content could.

After a while, nonetheless, I asked him whether he had perhaps something to say to me; I should gladly go to one side with him and talk over his concern. He vigorously declined. The conversation began again and with it M.'s listening. When another half hour had passed, I asked him again whether he did not perhaps have a wish that I might fulfill for him; he could count on me. No, no, he had no wish, he assured me. It had grown late; but, as happens to one in such hours of lively interchange, I did not feel weary; I felt fresher, in fact, than before, and decided to go for a walk with the young people. At this moment M. approached me with an unspeakably timid air. "Doctor," he said, "I should like to ask you a question." I bid the students wait and sat down with him at a table. He was silent. "Just ask, Mr. M.," I encouraged him; "I shall gladly give you information as best I can." "Doctor," he said, "I have a daughter." He paused; then he continued, "And I also have a young man for my daughter." Again a pause. "He is a student of law. He passed the examinations with distinction." He paused again, this time somewhat longer. I looked at him encouragingly; I supposed that he would entreat me to use my influence in some way on behalf of the presumptive son-in-law. "Doctor," he asked, "is he a steady man?" I was surprised, but felt that I might not refuse him an answer. "Now, Mr. M.," I explained, "after what you have said, it can certainly be taken for granted that he is industrious and able." Still he questioned further. "But Doctor," he said, "does he also have a good head?"—"That is even more difficult to answer," I replied; "but at any rate he has not succeeded with industry alone, he must also have something in his head." Once again M. paused; then he asked, clearly as a final question, "Doctor, should he now become a judge or a lawyer?"—"About that I can give you no information," I answered. "I do not know the young man, indeed, and even if I did know him, I should hardly be able to advise in this matter." But then M. regarded me with a glance of almost melancholy renunciation, half-complaining, half-understanding, and spoke in an indescribable tone, composed in equal part of sorrow and humility: "Doctor, you do not *want* to say—now, I thank you for what you have said to me."

This humorous and meaningful occurrence, which apparently has nothing to do with Hasidism, afforded me, nonetheless, a new and significant insight into it. As a child, I had received an image of the zaddik and through the sullied reality had glimpsed the pure idea, the idea of the genuine leader of a genuine community. Between youth and manhood this idea had arisen in me through knowledge of Hasidic teaching as that of the perfected man who realizes God in the world. But now in the light of this droll event, I caught sight in my inner experience of the zaddik's function as a leader. I, who am truly no zaddik, no one assured in God, rather a man endangered before God, a man wrestling ever anew for God's light, ever anew engulfed in God's abysses, nonetheless, when asked a trivial question and replying with a trivial answer, then experienced from within for the first time the true zaddik, questioned about revelations and replying in revelations. I experienced him in the fundamental relation of his soul to the world: in his responsibility.

Each man has an infinite sphere of responsibility, responsibility before the infinite. He moves, he talks, he looks, and each of his movements, each of his words, each of his glances causes waves to surge in the happening of the world: he cannot know how strong and how far-reaching. Each man with all his being and doing determines the fate of the world in a measure unknowable to him and all others; for the causality which we can perceive is indeed only a tiny segment of the inconceivable, manifold, invisible working of all upon all. Thus every human action is a vessel of infinite responsibility.

But there are men who are hourly accosted by infinite responsibility in a special, specially active form. I do not mean the rulers and statesmen who have to determine the external destiny of great communities; their sphere of action is all-embracing but, in order to be effective, they turn away from the individual, enormously threatened lives that glance at them with thousandfold question, to the general that appears to them unseeing. I mean those who withstand the thousandfold-questioning glance of individual lives, who give true answer to the trembling mouth of the needy creature who time after time demands from them decision; I mean the zaddikim, I mean the true zaddik. That is the man who hourly measures the depths of responsibility with the sounding lead of his words. He speaks—and knows that his speech is destiny. He does not decide the fate of countries and peoples, but ever again only the small and great course of an individual life, so finite and yet so boundless. Men come to him, and each desires his opinion, his help. And even though [illegible] corporal and semi-corporal needs that they bring to him, in his world-insight there is nothing corporal that cannot be transfigured, nothing material that cannot be raised to spirit. And it is this that he does for all: *he elevates their need before he satisfies it.*

Thus he is the helper in spirit, the teacher of world-meaning, the conveyor to the divine sparks. The world needs him, the perfected man; it awaits him, it awaits him ever again.

BOOK 

THE LIFE OF THE HASIDIM

HITLAHAVUT: ECSTASY

Hitlahavut is "the inflaming," the ardor of ecstasy. It is the goblet of grace and the eternal key.

A fiery sword guards the way to the tree of life. It scatters into sparks before the touch of hitlahavut, whose light finger is more powerful than it. To hitlahavut the path is open, and all bounds sink before its boundless step. The world is no longer its place: it is the place of the world.

Hitlahavut unlocks the meaning of life. Without it even heaven has no meaning and no being. "If a man has fulfilled the whole of the teaching and all the commandments but has not had the rapture and the inflaming, when he dies and passes beyond, paradise is opened to him but, because he has not felt rapture in the world, he also does not feel it in paradise."

Hitlahavut: Ecstasy

Hitlahavut can appear at all places and at all times. Each hour is its footstool and each deed its throne. Nothing can stand against it, nothing hold it down; nothing can defend itself against its might, which raises everything corporeal to spirit. He who is in it is in holiness. "He can speak idle words with his mouth, yet the teaching of the Lord is in his heart at this hour; he can pray in a whisper, yet his heart cries out in his breast; he can sit in a community of men, yet he walks with God: mixing with the creatures yet secluded from the world." Each thing and each deed is thus sanctified. "When a man attaches himself to God, he can allow his mouth to speak what it may speak and his ear to hear what it may hear, and he will bind the things to their higher root."

Repetition, the power which weakens and decolors so much in human life, is powerless before ecstasy, which catches fire again and again from precisely the most regular, most uniform events. Ecstasy overcame one zaddik in reciting the Scriptures, each time that he reached the words, "And God spoke." A Hasidic wise man who told this to his disciples added to it, "But I think also: if one speaks in truth and one receives in truth, then one word is enough to uplift the whole world and to purge the whole world from sin." To the man in ecstasy the habitual is eternally new. A zaddik stood at the window in the early morning light and trembling cried, "A few hours ago it was night and now it is day—God brings up the day!" And he was full of fear and trembling. He also said, "Every creature should be ashamed before the Creator: were he perfect, as he was destined to be, then he would be astonished and awakened and inflamed because of the renewal of the creature at each time and in each moment."

But hitlahavut is not a sudden sinking into eternity: it is an ascent to the infinite from rung to rung. To find God means to find the way without end. The Hasidim saw the "world to come" in the image of this way, and they never called that world a Beyond. One of the pious saw a dead master in a dream. The latter told him that from the hour of his death he went each day from world to world. And the world which yesterday was stretched out above his gaze as heaven is today the earth under his foot; and the heaven of today is the earth of tomorrow. And each world is purer and more beautiful and more profound than the one before.

The angel rests in God, but the holy spirits go forward in God. "The angel is one who stands, and the holy man is one who travels on. Therefore the holy man is higher than the angel."

Such is the way of ecstasy. If it appears to offer an end, an arriving, an attaining, an acquiring, it is only a final no, not a final yes: it is the end of constraint, the shaking off of the last chains, the detachment which is lifted above everything earthly. "When man moves from strength to strength and ever upward and upward until he comes to the root of all teaching and all command, to the I of God, the simple unity and boundlessness —when he stands there, then all the wings of command and law sink down and are as if destroyed. For the evil impulse is destroyed since he stands above it."

"Above nature and above time and above thought"—thus is he called who is in ecstasy. He has cast off all sorrow and all that is oppressive. "Sweet suffering, I receive you in love," said a dying zaddik, and Rabbi Susya cried out amazed when his hand slipped out of the fire in which he had placed it, "How coarse Susya's body has become that it is afraid of fire." The man of ecstasy rules life, and no external happening that penetrates into his realm can disturb his inspiration. It is told of a zaddik that when the holy meal of the teaching prolonged itself till morning, he said to his disciples, "We have not stepped into the limits of the day, rather the day has stepped into our limits, and we need not give way before it."

In ecstasy all that is past and that is future draws near to the present. Time shrinks, the line between the eternities disappears, only the moment lives, and the moment is eternity. In its undivided light appears all that was and all that will be, simple and composed. It is there as a heartbeat is there and becomes manifest like it.

The Hasidic legend has much to tell of those wonderful ones who remembered their earlier forms of existence, who were aware of the future as of their own breath, who saw from one end of the earth to the other and felt all the changes that took place in the world as something that happened to their own bodies. All this is not yet that state in which hitlahavut has overcome the world of space and time. We can perhaps learn something of this latter state from two simple anecdotes which supplement each other. It is told of one master that he had to look at a clock during the hour of withdrawal in order to keep himself in this world; and of another that when he wished to observe individual things he had to put on spectacles in order to restrain his spiritual vision; "for otherwise he saw all the individual things of the world as one."

But the highest rung which is reported is that

in which the withdrawn one transcends his own ecstasy. When a disciple once remarked that a zaddik had "grown cold" and censored him for it, he was instructed by another, "There is a very high holiness; if one enters it, one becomes detached from all being and can no longer become inflamed." Thus ecstasy completes itself in its own suspension.

At times it expresses itself in an action that it consecrates and fills with holy meaning. The purest form—that in which the whole body serves the aroused soul and in which each of the soul's risings and bendings creates a visible symbol corresponding to it, allowing one image of enraptured meaning to emerge out of a thousand waves of movement—is the dance. It is told of the dancing of one zaddik, "His foot was as light as that of a four-year-old child. And among all who saw his holy dancing, there was not one in whom the holy turning was not accomplished, for in the hearts of all who saw he worked both weeping and rapture in one." Or the soul lays hold of the voice of a man and makes it sing what the soul has experienced in the heights, and the voice does not know what it does. Thus one zaddik stood in prayer in the "days of awe" (New Year and the Day of Atonement) and sang new melodies, "wonder of wonder, that he had never heard and that no human ear had ever heard, and he did not know at all what he sang and in what way he sang, for he was bound to the upper world."

But the truest life of the man of ecstasy is not among men. It is said of one master that he behaved like a stranger, according to the words of David the King: A sojourner am I in the land. "Like a man who comes from afar, from the city of his birth. He does not think of honors nor of anything for his own welfare; he only thinks about returning home to the city of his birth. He can possess nothing, for he knows: That is alien, and I must go home." Many walk in solitude, in "the wandering." Rabbi Susya used to stride about in the woods and sing songs of praise with such great ardor "that one would almost say that he was out of his mind." Another was only to be found in the streets and gardens and groves. When his father-in-law reproved him for this, he answered with the parable of the hen who hatched out goose eggs, "And when she saw her children swimming about on the surface of the water, she ran up and down in consternation seeking help for the unfortunate ones; and did not understand that this was their whole life to them: to roam there on the surface of the water."

There are still more profoundly solitary ones whose hitlahavut, for all that, is not yet fulfilled.

They become "unsettled and fugitive." They go into exile in order "to suffer exile with the Shekina." It is one of the basic conceptions of the Kabbala that the Shekina, the exiled glory of God, wanders endlessly, separated from her "lord," and that she will be reunited with him only in the hour of redemption. So these men of ecstasy wander over the earth, dwelling in the silent distances of God's exile, companions of the universal and holy happening of existence. The man who is detached in this way is the friend of God, "as a stranger is the friend of another stranger on account of their strangeness on earth." There are moments in which he sees the Shekina face to face in human form, as that zaddik saw it in the holy land "in the shape of a woman who weeps and laments over the husband of her youth."

But not only in faces out of the dark and in the silence of wandering does God give Himself to the soul afire with Him. Rather out of all the things of the earth His eye looks into the eye of him who seeks, and every being is the fruit in which He offers Himself to the yearning soul. Being is unveiled in the hand of the holy man. "The soul of him who longs very much for a woman and regards her many-colored garment is not turned to its gorgeous material and its colors but to the splendor of the longed-for woman who is clothed in it. But the others see only the garment and no more. So he who in truth longs for and embraces God sees in all the things of the world only the strength and the pride of the Creator who lives in the things. But he who is not on this rung sees the things as separate from God."

This is the earthly life of hitlahavut which soars beyond all limits. It enlarges the soul to the all. It narrows the all down to nothing. A Hasidic master speaks of it in words of mystery: "The creation of heaven and of earth is the unfolding of something out of nothing, the descent of the higher into the lower. But the holy men who detach themselves from being and ever cleave to God see and comprehend Him in truth, as if in the nothing before creation. They turn the something back into nothing. And this is the more wonderful: to raise up what is beneath. As it is written in the Gemara: The last wonder is greater than the first."

AVODA: SERVICE

Hitlahavut is envelopment in God beyond time and space. *Avoda* is the service of God in time and space.

Hitlahavut is the mystic meal. Avoda is the mystic offering.

These are the poles between which the life of the holy man swings.

Hitlahavut is silent since it lies on the heart of God. Avoda speaks, "What am I and what is my life that I wish to offer you my blood and my fire?"

Hitlahavut is as far from avoda as fulfillment is from longing. And yet hitlahavut streams out of avoda as the finding of God from the seeking of God.

The Baal-Shem told, "A king once built a great and glorious palace with numberless chambers, but only one door was opened. When the building was finished, it was announced that all princes should appear before the king who sat enthroned in the last of the chambers. But when they entered, they saw that there were doors open on all sides which led to winding passages in the distance, and there were again doors and again passages, and no end arose before the bewildered eyes. Then came the king's son and saw that all the labyrinth was a mirrored illusion, and he saw his father sitting in the hall before him."

The mystery of grace cannot be interpreted. Between seeking and finding lies the tension of a human life, indeed the thousandfold return of the anxious, wandering soul. And yet the flight of a moment is slower than the fulfillment. For God wishes to be sought, and how could he not wish to be found?

When the holy man brings ever new fire that the glowing embers on the altar of his soul may not be extinguished, God Himself says the sacrificial speech.

God governs men as He governed chaos at the time of the infancy of the world. "And as when the world began to unfold and He saw that if it flowed further asunder it would no longer be able to return home to its roots, then he spoke, 'Enough!'—

so it is that when the soul of man in its suffering rushes headlong, without direction, and evil becomes so mighty in it that it soon could no longer return home, then His compassion awakens, and he says, 'Enough!' "

But man too can say "Enough!" to the multiplicity within him. When he collects himself and becomes one, he draws near to the oneness of God —he serves his Lord. This is avoda.

It was said of one zaddik, "With him, teaching and prayer and eating and sleeping are all one, and he can raise the soul to its root."

All action bound in one and the infinite life carried into every action: this is avoda. "In all the deeds of man—speaking and looking and listening and going and remaining standing and lying down —the boundless is clothed."

From every deed an angel is born, a good angel or a bad one. But from half-hearted and confused deeds which are without meaning or without power angels are born with twisted limbs or without a head or hands or feet.

When through all action the rays of the universal sun radiate and the light concentrates in every deed, this is service. But no special act is elected for this service. God wills that one serve Him in all ways.

"There are two kinds of love: the love of a man

for his wife, which ought properly to express itself in secret and not where spectators are, for this love can only fulfill itself in a place secluded from the creatures; and the love for brothers and sisters and for children, which needs no concealment. Similarly, there are two kinds of love for God: the love through the teaching and prayer and the fulfillment of the commandments—this love ought properly to be consummated in silence and not in public, in order that it may not tempt one to glory and pride—and the love in the time when one mixes with the creatures, when one speaks and hears, gives and takes with them, and yet in the secret of one's heart one cleaves to God and does not cease to think of Him. And this is a higher rung than that, and of it it is said, 'Oh, that thou wert as my brother that sucked on the breasts of my mother! When I should find thee without I would kiss thee; yea, and none would despise me.' "

This is not to be understood, however, as if there were in this kind of service a cleavage between the earthly and the heavenly deed. Rather each motion of the surrendered soul is a vessel of holiness and of power. It is told of one zaddik that he had so sanctified all his limbs that each step of his feet wed worlds to one another. "Man is a ladder, placed on earth and touching heaven with its head.

And all his gestures and affairs and speaking leave traces in the higher world."

Here the inner meaning of avoda is intimated, coming from the depths of the old Jewish secret teaching and illuminating the mystery of that duality of ecstasy and service, of having and seeking.

God has fallen into duality through the created world and its deed: into the essence of God, Elohim, which is withdrawn from the creatures, and the presence of God, the Shekina, which dwells in things, wandering, straying, scattered. Only redemption will reunite the two in eternity. But it is given to the human spirit, through its service, to be able to bring the Shekina near to its source, to help it to enter it. And in this moment of homecoming, before it must again descend into the being of things, the whirlpool which rushes through the life of the stars becomes silent, the torches of the great devastation are extinguished, the whip in the hand of fate drops down, the world-pain pauses and listens: the grace of graces has appeared, blessing pours down out of infinity. Until the power of entanglement begins to drag down the Shekina and all becomes as before.

This is the meaning of service. Only the prayer that takes place for the sake of the Shekina truly lives. "Through his need and his want he knows the want of the Shekina, and he prays that the want of the Shekina will be satisfied and that through him, the praying man, the unification of God with His presence will take place." Man should know that his suffering comes from the suffering of the Shekina. He is "one of her limbs," and the stilling of her need is the only true stilling of his. "He does not think about the satisfaction of his needs, neither the lower nor the higher ones, that he might not be like him who cuts off the eternal plants and causes separation. Rather he does all for the sake of the want of the Shekina, and all will be resolved of itself, and his own suffering too will be stilled out of the stilling of the higher roots. For all, above and below, is one unity." "I am prayer," speaks the Shekina. A zaddik said, "Men think they pray before God, but it is not so, for prayer itself is divinity."

In the narrow room of self no prayer can thrive. "He who prays in suffering because of the melancholy which governs him and thinks that he prays in fear of God, or he who prays in joy because of the brightness of his mood and thinks he prays in love of God—his prayer is nothing at all. For this fear is only melancholy and this love is only empty joy."

It is told that the Baal-Shem once remained

standing on the threshold of a house of prayer and did not want to enter. He spoke in aversion: "I cannot enter there. The house is full to the brim of teaching and prayer." And when his companions were astonished, because it appeared to them that there could be no greater praise than this, he explained to them, "During the day the people speak here words without true devotion, without love and compassion, words that have no wings. They remain between the walls, they squat on the floor, they grow layer by layer like decaying leaves until the decay has packed the house to overflowing and there is no longer room for me in there."

Prayer may be held down in two different ways: if it is spoken without inner intention and if the earlier deeds of the praying man spread themselves like a thick cloud between him and heaven. The obstacle can only be overcome if the man grows upward into the sphere of ecstasy and purifies himself in its grace, or if another soul who is in ecstasy sets the fettered prayers free and carries them upward along with his own. Thus it is told of one zaddik that he stood for a long time silent and without movement during communal prayer and only then began himself to pray, "just as the tribe of Dan lay at the end of the camp and gathered all that was lost." His word became a garment to whose folds the prayers that were held below would cling and be borne upward. This zaddik used to say of prayer, "I bind myself with the whole of Israel, with those who are greater than I that through them my thoughts may ascend, and with those who are lesser than I that they may be uplifted through me."

But this is the mystery of community: not only do the lower need the higher, but the higher also need the lower. Here lies another distinction between the state of ecstasy and the state of service. Hitlahavut is the individual way and goal; a rope is stretched over the abyss, tied to two slender trees shaken by the storm: it is trod in solitude and dread by the foot of the venturer. Here there is no human community, neither in doubt nor in attainment. Service, however, is open to many souls in union. The souls bind themselves to one another for greater unity and might. There is a service that only the community can fulfill.

The Baal-Shem told a parable: "Some men stood under a very high tree. And one of the men had eyes to see. He saw that in the top of the tree stood a bird, glorious with genuine beauty. But the others did not see it. And a great longing came over the man to reach the bird and take it; and he could not go from there without the bird. But because of the height of the tree this was not in his power, and a ladder was not to be found. Still out of his great and powerful longing he found a way. He took the men who stood around him and placed them on top of one another, each on the shoulder of a comrade. He, however, climbed to the top so that he reached the bird and took it. And although the men had helped him, they knew nothing of the bird and did not see it. But he, who knew it and saw it, would not have been able to reach it without them. If, moreover, the lowest of them had left his place, then those above would have fallen to the earth. 'And the Temple of the Messiah is called the bird's nest in the book Zohar.' "

But it is not as if only the zaddik's prayer is received by God or as if only this prayer is lovely in His eyes. No prayer is stronger in grace and penetrates in more direct flight through all the worlds of heaven than that of the simple man who does not know anything to say and only knows to offer God the unbroken promptings of his heart. God receives them as a king receives the singing of a nightingale in his gardens at night, a singing that sounds sweeter to him than the homage of the princes in his throne room. The Hasidic legend cannot give enough examples of the favor that shines on the undivided person and of the power of his service. One of these we shall set down here.

Avoda: Service

A villager who year after year attended the prayer house of the Baal-Shem in the "days of awe" had a boy who was dull in understanding and could not even learn the shape of the letters, let alone understand the holy words. The father did not take him to the city on the "days of awe," for he knew nothing. Still when he was thirteen years old and of age to receive God's law, the father took him with him on the Day of Atonement that he might not eat something on the day of penance through lack of knowledge and understanding. Now the boy had a little whistle on which he always whistled during the time when he sat in the field and pastured the sheep and calves. He had brought it with him in his pocket without his father's knowing it. The boy sat in the prayer house during the holy hours and did not know anything to say. But when the Mussaf prayer was begun, he spoke to his father, "Father, I have my whistle with me, and I wish to play on it."

Then the father was very disturbed and commanded him, "Take care that you do not do so."

And he had to hold himself in. But when the Mincha prayer came, he spoke again: "Father, allow me now to take my whistle."

When the father saw that his soul desired to whistle, he became angry and asked him, "Where do you keep it?" and when the boy showed him the place, he laid his hand on the pocket and held it over it from then on to guard the whistle. But the Neila prayer began, and the lights burned trembling in the evening, and the hearts burned like the lights, unexhausted by the long waiting. And through the house the eighteen benedictions strode once again, weary but erect. And the great confession returned for the last time and, before the evening descended and God judged, lay yet once more before the ark of the Lord, its forehead on the floor and its hands extended. Then the boy could no longer suppress his ecstasy; he tore the whistle from his pocket and let its voice powerfully resound. All stood startled and bewildered. But the Baal-Shem raised himself above them and spoke, "The judgment is suspended, and wrath is dispelled from the face of the earth."

Thus every service which proceeds from a simple or a unified soul is sufficient and complete. But there is a still higher one. For he who has ascended from avoda to hitlahavut has submerged his will in it and receives his deed from it alone, having risen above every separate service. "Each zaddik has his special way of serving. But when the zaddik contemplates his root and attains to the Nothing, then he can serve God on all rungs."

Thus one of them said, "I stand before God as a messenger boy." For he had attained to completion and to the Nothing so that he no longer possessed any special way. "Rather he stood ready for all ways which God might show him, as a messenger boy stands ready for all that his master will command him." He who thus serves in perfection has conquered the primeval duality and has brought hitlahavut into the heart of avoda. He dwells in the kingdom of life, and yet all walls have fallen, all boundary-stones are uprooted, all separation is destroyed. He is the brother of the creatures and feels their glance as if it were his own, their step as if his own feet walked, their blood as if it flowed through his own body. He is the son of God and lays his soul anxiously and securely in the great hand beside all the heavens and earths and unknown worlds, and stands on the flood of the sea into which all his thoughts and the wanderings of all beings flow. "He makes his body the throne of life and life the throne of the spirit and the spirit the throne of the soul and the soul the throne of the light of God's glory, and the light streams round about him, and he sits in the midst of the light and trembles and rejoices."

KAVANA: INTENTION

K*avana* is the mystery of a soul directed to a goal.

Kavana is not will. It does not think of transplanting an image into the world of actual things, of making fast a dream as an object so that it may be at hand, to be experienced at one's convenience in satiating recurrence. Nor does it desire to throw the stone of action into the well of happening that its waters may for a while become troubled and astonished, only to return then to the deep command of their existence, nor to lay a spark on the fuse that runs through the succession of the generations, that a flame may jump from age to age until it is extinguished in one of them without sign or leave-taking. Not this is Kavana's meaning, that the horses pulling the great wagon should feel one impulse more or that one building more should be erected beneath the overfull gaze of the stars. Kavana does not mean purpose but goal.

But there are no *goals*, only *the goal*. There is only one goal that does not lie, that becomes entangled in no new way, only one into which all ways flow, before which no byway can forever flee: redemption.

Kavana is a ray of God's glory that dwells in each man and means redemption.

This is redemption, that the Shekina shall return home from its exile. "That all shells may withdraw from God's glory and that it may purify itself and unite itself with its owner in perfect unity." As a sign of this the Messiah will appear and make all beings free.

To many a Hasid it is, for the whole of his life, as if this must happen here and now. For he hears the voice of becoming roaring in the gorges and feels the seed of eternity in the ground of time as if it were in his blood. And so he can never think otherwise than that *this* moment and now *this* one will be the chosen moment. And his imagination compels him ever more fervently, for ever more commandingly speaks the voice and ever more demandingly swells the seed.

It is told of one zaddik that he awaited redemption with such eagerness that when he heard a tumult in the street, he was at once moved to ask what it was and whether the messenger had not come; and each time that he went to sleep he commanded his servant to awaken him at the very moment when the messenger came. "For the coming of the redeemer was so deeply implanted in his heart that it was as when a father awaits his only son from a distant land and stands on the watch-tower with longing in his eyes and peers through all the windows and, when one opens the door, hurries out to see whether his son has not come." Others, however, are aware of the progress of the stride, see the place and hour of the path and know the distance of the Coming One. Each thing shows them the uncompleted state of the world, the need of existence speaks to them, and the breath of the winds bears bitterness to them. The world in their eyes is like an unripe fruit. Inwardly they partake in the glory—then they look outward: all lies in battle.

When the great zaddik Rabbi Menachem was in Jerusalem, it happened that a foolish man climbed the Mount of Olives and blew the shofar trumpet. No one had seen him. A rumor spread among the people that this was the shofar blast which announced the redemption. When this came to the ears of the rabbi, he opened a window and looked out into the air of the world. And he said at once, "Here is no renewal."

This is the way of redemption: that all souls and all sparks of souls which have sprung from the primeval soul and have sunk and become scattered in all creatures at the time of the original darkening of the world or through the guilt of the ages should conclude their wandering and return home purified. The Hasidim speak of this in the parable of the prince who allows the meal to begin only when the last of the guests has entered.

All men are the abode of wandering souls. These dwell in many creatures and strive from form to form toward perfection. But those which are not able to purify themselves are caught in the "world of confusion" and make their homes in lakes of water, in stones, in plants, in animals, awaiting the redeeming hour.

It is not only souls that are everywhere imprisoned but also sparks of souls. No thing is without them. They live in all that is. Each form is their prison.

And this is the meaning and mission of kavana: that it is given to men to lift up the fallen and to free the imprisoned. Not only to wait, not only to watch for the Coming One: man can work toward the redemption of the world.

Just that is kavana: the mystery of the soul that is directed to redeem the world.

It is told of some holy men that they imagined that they might bring about redemption by storm and force—in this world, when they were so afire with the grace of ecstasy that to them, who had even embraced God, nothing appeared unattainable any longer, or in the coming world. A dying zaddik said, "My friends have gone hence, intending to bring the Messiah, and have forgotten to do so in their rapture. But I shall not forget."

In reality, however, each can only be effective in his domain. Each man has a sphere of being, far extended in space and time, which is allotted to him to be redeemed through him. Places which are heavy with unraised sparks and in which souls are fettered wait for the man who will come to them with the word of freedom. When a hasid cannot pray in one place and goes to another, then the first place demands of him, "Why would you not speak the holy words over me? And if there is evil in me, then it is for you to redeem me." But also all journeys have secret destinations of which the traveler is unaware.

It was said of some zaddikim that they had a

helping power over the wandering souls. At all times, but especially when they stood in prayer, the wanderers of eternity appeared imploring before them, wishing to receive salvation from their hands. But they also knew how to find the voiceless among the banished in the exile of a tired body or in the darkness of the elements and to upraise them.

This help is an awesome venture, set down in the midst of threatening dangers, which only the holy man can enter upon without going under. "He who has a soul may let himself down into the abyss, bound fast to the rim above through his thoughts, as through a strong rope, and will return. But he who only has life or only life and spirit, he who has not yet attained the rung of thought, for him the bond will not hold and he will fall into the depths."

But, though it is only those blessed ones who can plunge tranquilly into the darkness in order to aid a soul which is abandoned to the whirlpool of wandering, it is not denied to even the least of persons to raise the lost sparks from their imprisonment and send them home.

The sparks are to be found everywhere. They are suspended in things as in sealed-off springs; they stoop in the creatures as in walled-up caves, they inhale darkness and they exhale dread; they wait. And those that dwell in space flit hither and thither around the movements of the world, like light-mad butterflies, looking to see which of them they might enter in order to be redeemed through them. They all wait expectantly for freedom.

"The spark in a stone or a plant or another creature is like a complete figure which sits in the middle of the thing as in a block, so that its hands and feet cannot stretch themselves and the head lies on the knees. He who is able to lift the holy spark leads this figure into freedom, and no setting free of captives is greater than this. It is as when a king's son is rescued from captivity and brought to his father."

But the liberation does not take place through formulae of exorcism or through any kind of prescribed and special action. All this grows out of the ground of otherness, which is not the ground of kavana. No leap from the everyday into the miraculous is required. "With his every act man can work on the figure of the glory of God that it may step forth out of its concealment." It is not the matter of the action, but only its dedication that is decisive. Just that which you do in the uniformity of recurrence or in the disposition of events, just this answer of the acting person to the manifold demands of the hour—an answer acquired through practice or won through inspiration—just this continuity of the living stream, when accomplished in dedication, leads to redemption. He who prays and sings in holiness, eats and speaks in holiness, in holiness takes the prescribed ritual bath and in holiness is mindful of his business, through him the fallen sparks are raised and the fallen worlds redeemed and renewed.

Around each man—enclosed within the wide sphere of his activity—is laid a natural circle of things which, before all, he is called to set free. These are the creatures and objects that are spoken of as the possessions of this individual: his animals and his walls, his garden and his meadow, his tools and his food. In so far as he cultivates and enjoys them in holiness, he frees their souls. "For this reason a man should always have mercy on his tools and all his possessions."

But also in the soul itself there appear those that need liberation. Most of these are sparks which have fallen through the guilt of this soul in one of its earlier lives. They are the alien, disturbing thoughts that often come to man in prayer. "When man stands in prayer and desires to join himself to the Eternal, and the alien thoughts come and descend on him, these are holy sparks that have sunken and that wish to be raised and redeemed by him; and the sparks belong to him, they are kindred to the roots of his soul: it is his power that will redeem them." He redeems them when he restores each troubled thought to its pure source, allows each impulse intent on a particular thing to flow into the divine creative impulse, allows everything alien to be submerged in the divine self-identity.

This is the kavana of receiving: that one redeem the sparks in the surrounding things and the sparks that draw near out of the invisible. But there is yet another kavana, the kavana of giving. It bears no stray soul-rays in helpful hands; it binds worlds to one another and rules over the mysteries, it pours itself into the thirsty distance, it gives itself to infinity. But it too has no need of miraculous deeds. Its path is creation, and the word before all other forms of creation.

From time immemorial speech was for the Jewish mystic a rare and awe-inspiring thing. A characteristic theory of letters existed which dealt with them as with the elements of the world and with their intermixture as with the inwardness of reality. The word is an abyss through which the speaker strides. "One should speak words as if the heavens were opened in them. And as if it were not so that you take the word in your mouth, but rather as if you entered into the word." He who knows the secret melody that bears the inner into the outer, who knows the holy song that merges the lonely, shy letters into the singing of the spheres, he is full of the power of God, "and it is as if he created heaven and earth and all worlds anew." He does not find his sphere before him as does the freer of souls, he extends it from the firmament to the silent depths. But he also works toward redemption. "For in each letter are the three: world, soul, and divinity. They rise and join and unite themselves, and they become the word, and the words unite themselves in God in genuine unity, since a man has set his soul in them, and worlds unite themselves and ascend, and the great rapture is born." Thus the acting person prepares the final oneness of all things.

And as avoda flowed into hitlahavut, the basic principle of Hasidic life, so here too kavana flows into hitlahavut. For creating means to be created: the divine moves and overcomes us. And to be created is ecstasy: only he who sinks into the Nothing of the Absolute receives the forming hand of the spirit. This is portrayed in parable. It is not given to anything in the world to be reborn and to attain to a new form unless it comes first to the Nothing, that is, to the "form of the in between." No creature can exist in it, it is the power before creation and is called chaos. Thus the perishing of the egg into the chick and thus the seed, which does not sprout before it has gone down into the earth and decayed. "And this is called wisdom, that is, a thought without revelation. And so it is: if man desires that a new creation come out of him, then he must come with all his potentiality to the state of nothing, and then God brings forth in him a new creation, and he is like a fountain that does not run dry and a stream that does not cease to flow."

Thus the will of the Hasidic teaching of kavana is twofold: that enjoyment, the internalizing of that which is without, should take place in holiness and that creation, the externalizing of that which is within, should take place in holiness. Through holy creation and through holy enjoyment the redemption of the world is accomplished.

SHIFLUT: HUMILITY

God never does the same thing twice, said Rabbi Nachman of Bratzlav.

That which exists is unique, and it happens but once. New and without a past, it emerges from the flood of returnings, takes place, and plunges back into it, unrepeatable. Each thing reappears at another time, but each transformed. And the throws and falls that rule over the great world-creations, and the water and fire which shape the form of the earth, and the mixings and unmixings which brew the life of the living, and the spirit of man with all its trial-and-error relation to the yielding abundance of the possible—none of these can create an identical thing nor bring back one of the things that have been sealed as belonging to the past. It is because things happen but once that the individual partakes in eternity. For the individual with his inextinguishable uniqueness is engraved in the heart of the all and lies forever in the lap of the timeless as he who has been created thus and not otherwise.

Uniqueness is thus the essential good of man that is given to him to unfold. And just this is the meaning of the return, that his uniqueness may become ever purer and more complete; and that in each new life the one who has returned may stand in ever more untroubled and undisturbed incomparability. For pure uniqueness and pure perfection are one, and he who has become so entirely individual that no otherness any longer has power over him or place in him has completed the journey and is redeemed and rests in God.

"Every man shall know and consider that in his qualities he is unique in the world and that none like him ever lived, for had there ever before been someone like him, then he would not have needed to exist. But each is in truth a new thing in the world, and he shall make perfect his special characteristics, for it is because they are not perfect that the coming of the Messiah tarries."

Only in his own way and not in any other can the one who strives perfect himself. "He who lays hold of the rung of his companion and lets go of his own rung, through him neither the one nor the other will be realized. Many acted like Rabbi Simeon ben Jochai and in their hands it did not turn out well, for they were not of the same nature as he but only acted as they saw him act out of his nature."

But as man seeks God in lonely fervor and yet there is a high service that only the community can fulfill, and as man accomplishes enormous things with his everyday actions, yet does not do so alone but needs for such action the world and the things in it, so the uniqueness of man proves itself in his life with others. For the more unique a man really is, so much the more can he give to the other and so much the more will he give him. And this is his one sorrow, that his giving is limited by the one who takes. For "the bestower is on the side of mercy and the receiver is on the side of rigor. And so it is with each thing. As when one pours out of a large vessel into a goblet: the vessel pours from out of its fullness, but the goblet limits the gift."

The individual sees God and embraces Him. The individual redeems the fallen worlds. And yet the individual is not a whole, but a part. And the purer and more perfect he is, so much the more intimately does he know that he is a part and so much the more actively there stirs in him the community of existence. That is the mystery of humility.

"Every man has a light over him, and when the

souls of two men meet, the two lights join each other and from them there goes forth one light. And this is called generation." To feel the universal generation as a sea and oneself as a wave, that is the mystery of humility.

But it is not humility when one "lowers himself too much and forgets that man can bring down an overflowing blessing on all the world through his words and his actions." This is called impure humility. "The greatest evil is when you forget that you are the son of a king." He is truly humble who feels the other as himself and himself in the other.

Haughtiness means to contrast oneself with others. The haughty man is not he who knows himself, but he who compares himself with others. No man can presume too much if he stands on his own ground since all the heavens are open to him and all worlds devoted to him. The man who presumes too much is the man who contrasts himself with others, who sees himself as higher than the humblest of things, who rules with measure and weights and pronounces judgment.

"If Messiah should come today," a zaddik said, "and say, 'You are better than the others,' then I would say to him, 'You are not Messiah.' "

The soul of the haughty lives without product and essence; it flutters and toils and is not blessed.

The thoughts whose real intent is not what is thought but themselves and their brilliance are shadows. The deed which has in mind not the goal but the profit has no body, only surface, no existence, only appearance. He who measures and weighs becomes empty and unreal like measure and weight. "In him who is full of himself there is no room for God."

It is told of one disciple that he went into seclusion and cut himself off from the things of the world in order to cling solely to the teaching and the service, and he sat alone fasting from Sabbath to Sabbath and learning and praying. But his mind, beyond all conscious purpose, was filled with pride in his action; it shone before his eyes and his fingers burned to lay it on his forehead like the diadem of the anointed. And so all his work fell to the lot of the "other side," and the divine had no share in it. But his heart drove him ever more strongly so that he remained unaware of his fallen state in which the demons played with his acts, and he imagined himself wholly possessed by God. Then it happened once that he leaned outside of himself and became aware of the mute and alienated things around him: Then understanding possessed him and he beheld his deeds piled up at the feet of a gigantic idol, and he beheld himself in the reeling emptiness, abandoned to the nameless. This much is told and no more.

But the humble man has the "drawing power." As long as a man sees himself above and before others, he has a limit, "and God cannot pour His holiness into him, for God is without limit." But when a man rests in himself as in nothing, he is not limited by any other thing, he is limitless and God pours His glory into him.

The humility which is meant here is no willed and practiced virtue. It is nothing but an inner being, feeling, and expressing. Nowhere in it is there a compulsion, nowhere a self-humbling, a self-restraining, a self-resolve. It is indivisible as the glance of a child and simple as a child's speech.

The humble man lives in each being and knows each being's manner and virtue. Since no one is to him "the other," he knows from within that none lacks some hidden value; knows that there "is no man who does not have his hour." For him, the colors of the world do not blend with one another, rather each soul stands before him in the majesty of its particular existence. "In each man there is a priceless treasure that is in no other. Therefore, one shall honor each man for the hidden value that only he and none of his comrades has."

"God does not look on the evil side," said one zaddik; "how should I dare to do so?"

He who lives in others according to the mystery of humility can condemn no one. "He who passes sentence on a man has passed it on himself."

He who separates himself from the sinner departs in guilt. But the saint can suffer for the sins of a man as for his own. Only living with the other is justice.

Living with the other as a form of knowing is justice. Living with the other as a form of being is love. For that feeling that is called love among men, the feeling of being near and of wishing to be near a few, is nothing other than a recollection from a heavenly life: "Those who sat next to one another in Paradise and were neighbors and relatives, they are also near to one another in this world." But in truth love is all-comprehensive and sustaining and is extended to all the living without selection and distinction. "How can you say of me that I am a leader of the generation," said a zaddik, "when I still feel in myself a stronger love for those near me and for my seed than for all men?" That this attitude also extends to animals is shown by the accounts of Rabbi Wolf who could never shout at a horse, of Rabbi Moshe Leib, who gave drink to the neglected calves at the market, of Rabbi Susya who could not see a cage, "and the wretchedness of the bird and its anxiety to fly in the air of the world and to be a free wanderer in accordance with its nature," without opening it. But it is not only the beings to whom the shortsighted gaze of the crowd accords the name of "living" who are embraced by the love of the loving man: "There is no thing in the world in which there is not life, and each has the form of life in which it stands before your eyes. And lo, this life is the life of God."

Thus it is held that the love of the living is love of God, and it is higher than any other service. A master asked one of his disciples, "You know that two forces cannot occupy the human mind at the same time. If then you rise from your couch tomorrow and two ways are before you: the love of God and the love of man, which should come first?" "I do not know," the latter answered. Then spoke the master, "It is written in the prayer book that is in the hands of the people, 'Before you pray, say the words, Love thy companion as one like thyself.' Do you think that the venerable ones commanded that without purpose? If someone says to you that he has love for God but has no love for the living, he speaks falsely and pretends that which is impossible."

Therefore, when one has departed from God, the

love of a man is his only salvation. When a father complained to the Baal-Shem, "My son is estranged from God—what shall I do?" he replied, "Love him more."

This is one of the primary Hasidic words: to love more. Its roots sink deep and stretch out far. He who has understood this can learn to understand Judaism anew. There is a great moving force therein.

A great moving force and yet again only a lost sound. It is a lost sound, when somewhere—in that dark windowless room—and at some time—in those days without the power of message—the lips of a nameless, soon-to-be-forgotten man, of the zaddik Rabbi Rafael, formed these words, "If a man sees that his companion hates him, he shall love him the more. For the community of the living is the carriage of God's majesty, and where there is a rent in the carriage, one must fill it, and where there is so little love that the joining comes apart, one must love more on one's own side to overcome the lack."

Once before a journey this Rabbi Rafael called to a disciple that he should sit beside him in the carriage. "I fear I shall make it too crowded for you," the latter responded. But the rabbi now spoke in a stronger voice, "So we shall love each other more: then there will be room enough for us."

They may stand here as a witness, the symbol and the reality, separate and yet one and inseparable, the carriage of the Shekina and the carriage of the friends.

It is the love of a being who lives in a kingdom greater than the kingdom of the individual and speaks out of a knowing deeper than the knowing of the individual. It exists in reality *between* the creatures, that is, it exists in God. Life covered and guaranteed by life, life pouring itself into life, thus first do you behold the soul of the world. What the one is wanting, the other makes up for. If one loves too little, the other will love more.

Things help one another. But helping means to do what one does for its own sake and with a collected will. As he who loves more does not preach love to the other, but himself loves and, in a certain sense, does not concern himself about the other, so the helping man, in a certain sense, does not concern himself about the other, but does what he does out of himself with the thought of helping. That means that the essential thing that takes place between beings does not take place through their intercourse, but through each seemingly isolated, seemingly unconcerned, seemingly unconnected action performed out of himself. This is said in parable: "If a man sings and cannot lift his voice and another comes to help him and begins to sing, then this one too can now lift his voice. And that is the secret of co-operation."

To help one another is no task, but a matter of course, the reality on which the life-together of the Hasidim is founded. Help is no virtue, but an artery of existence. That is the new meaning of the old Jewish saying that good deeds save one from death. It is commanded that the helping person not think about the others who could assist him, about God and man. He must not think of himself as a partial power that needs only to contribute; rather each must answer and be responsible for the whole. And one thing more, and this is again nothing other than an expression of the mystery of shiflut: not to help out of pity, that is, out of a sharp, quick pain which one wishes to expel, but out of love, that is, out of living with the other. He who pities does not live with the suffering of the sufferer, he does not bear it in his heart as one bears the life of a tree with all its drinking in and shooting forth and with the dream of its roots and the craving of its trunk and the thousand journeys of its branches, or as one bears the life of an animal with all its gliding, stretching, and grasping and all the joy of its sinews and its joints and the dull tension of its brain. He does not bear in his heart this special essence, the suffering of the other; rather he receives from the most external features of this suffering a sharp, quick pain, unbridgeably dissimilar to the original pain of the sufferer. And it is thus that he is moved. But the helper must live with the other, and only help that arises out of living with the other can stand before the eyes of God. Thus it is told of one zaddik that when a poor person had excited his pity, he provided first for all his pressing need, but then, when he looked inward and perceived that the wound of pity was healed, he plunged with great, restful, and devoted love into the life and needs of the other, took hold of them as if they were his own life and needs and began in reality to help.

He who lives with others in this way realizes with his deed the truth that all souls are one; for each is a spark from the original soul, and the whole of the original soul is in each.

Thus lives the humble man, who is the loving man and the helper: mixing with all and untouched by all, devoted to the multitude and collected in his uniqueness, fulfilling on the rocky summits of solitude the bond with the infinite and in the valley of life the bond with the earthly, flowering out of deep devotion and withdrawn from all desire of the desiring. He knows that all is in God and greets His messengers as trusted friends. He has no fear of the before and the after, of the above and the below, of this world and the world to come. He is at home and never can be cast out. The earth cannot help but be his cradle, and heaven cannot help but be his mirror and his echo.

THE WAY OF MAN ACCORDING TO THE TEACHINGS OF HASIDISM

INTRODUCTION

In most systems of belief the believer considers that he can achieve a perfect relationship to God by renouncing the world of the senses and overcoming his own natural being. Not so the hasid. Certainly, "cleaving" unto God is to him the highest aim of the human person, but to achieve it he is not required to abandon the external and internal reality of earthly being, but to affirm it in its true, God-oriented essence and thus so to transform it that he can offer it up to God.

Hasidism is no pantheism. It teaches the absolute transcendence of God, but as combined with his conditioned immanence. The world is an irradiation of God, but as it is endowed with an independence of existence and striving, it is apt, always and everywhere, to form a crust around itself. Thus, a divine spark lives in every thing and being, but each such spark is enclosed by an isolating shell. Only man can liberate it and re-join it with the Origin: by holding holy converse with the thing and using it in a holy manner, that is, so that his intention in doing so remains directed toward God's transcendence. Thus the divine immanence emerges from the exile of the "shells."

But also in man, in every man, is a force divine. And in man far more than in all other beings it can pervert itself, can be misused by himself. This happens if he, instead of directing it toward its origin, allows it to run directionless and seize at everything that offers itself to it; instead of hallowing passion, he makes it evil. But here, too, a way to redemption is open: he who with the entire force of his being "turns" to God, at this his point of the universe lifts the divine immanence out of its debasement, which he has caused.

The task of man, of every man, according to hasidic teaching, is to affirm for God's sake the world and himself and by this very means to transform both.

I. HEART-SEARCHING

Rabbi Shneur Zalman, the *rav** of Northern White Russia (died 1813), was put in jail in Petersburg, because the *mitnagdim*** had denounced his principles and his way of living to the government. He was awaiting trial when the chief of the gendarmes entered his cell. The majestic and quiet face of the rav, who was so deep in meditation that he did not at first notice his visitor, suggested to the chief, a thoughtful person, what manner of man he had before him. He began to converse with his prisoner and brought up a number of questions which had occurred to him in reading the Scriptures. Finally he asked: "How are we to understand that God, the all-knowing, said to Adam: 'Where art thou?' "

* Rabbi.

** adversaries (of Hasidism).

"Do you believe," answered the rav, "that the Scriptures are eternal and that every era, every generation and every man is included in them?"

"I believe this," said the other.

"Well then," said the zaddik, "in every era, God calls to every man: 'Where are you in your world? So many years and days of those allotted to you have passed, and how far have you gotten in your world?' God says something like this: 'You have lived forty-six years. How far along are you?' "

When the chief of the gendarmes heard his age mentioned, he pulled himself together, laid his hand on the rav's shoulder, and cried: "Bravo!" But his heart trembled.

What happens in this tale?

At first sight, it reminds us of certain Talmudic stories in which a Roman or some other heathen questions a Jewish sage about a Biblical passage, with a view to exposing an alleged contradiction in Jewish religious doctrine, and receives a reply which either explains that there is no such contradiction or refutes the questioner's arguments in some other way; sometimes, a personal admonition is added to the actual reply. But we soon perceive an important difference between those Talmudic stories and this Hasidic one, though at first the difference appears greater than it actually is. It consists in the fact that in the Hasidic story the reply is given on a different plane from that on which the question is asked.

The chief wants to expose an alleged contradiction in Jewish doctrine. The Jews profess to believe in God as the all-knowing, but the Bible makes him ask questions as they are asked by someone who wants to learn something he does not know. God seeks Adam, who has hidden himself. He calls into the garden, asking where he is; it would thus seem that He does not know it, that it is possible to hide from Him and, consequently, that He is not all-knowing. Now, instead of explaining the passage and solving the seeming contradiction, the rabbi takes the text merely as a starting point from where he proceeds to reproach the chief with his past life, his lack of seriousness, his thoughtlessness and irresponsibility. An impersonal question which, however seriously it may be meant in the present instance, is in fact no genuine question but merely a form of controversy, calls forth a personal reply or, rather, a personal admonition in lieu of a reply. It thus seems as if nothing had remained of those Talmudic answers but the admonition which sometimes accompanied them.

But let us examine the story more closely. The chief inquires about a passage from the Biblical story of Adam's sin. The rabbi's answer means, in effect: "You yourself are Adam, you are the man whom God asks: 'Where art thou?' " It would thus seem that the answer gives no explanation of the passage as such. In fact, however, it illuminates both the situation of the Biblical Adam and that of every man in every time and in every place. For as soon as the chief hears and understands that the Biblical question is addressed to him, he is bound to realize what it means when God asks: "Where art thou?" whether the question be addressed to Adam or to some other man. In so asking, God does not expect to learn something he does not know; what he wants is to produce an effect in man which can only be produced by just such a question, provided that it reaches man's heart—that man allows it to reach his heart.

Adam hides himself to avoid rendering accounts, to escape responsibility for his way of living. Every man hides for this purpose, for every man is Adam and finds himself in Adam's situation. To escape responsibility for his life, he turns existence into a system of hideouts. And in thus hiding again and again "from the face of God," he enmeshes himself more and more deeply in perversity. A new situation thus arises, which becomes more and more questionable with every day, with every new hide-out. This situation can be precisely defined as follows: Man cannot escape the eye of God, but in trying to hide from Him, he is hiding from himself. True, in him too there is something that seeks him, but he makes it harder and harder for that "something" to find him. This is the situation into which God's question falls. This question is designed to awaken man and destroy his system of hideouts; it is to show man to what pass he has come and to awake in him the great will to get out of it.

Everything now depends on whether man faces the question. Of course, every man's heart, like that of the chief in the story, will tremble when he hears it. But his system of hideouts will help to overcome this emotion. For the Voice does not come in a thunderstorm which threatens man's very existence; it is a "still small voice," and easy to drown. So long as this is done, man's life will not become a *way*. Whatever success and enjoyment he may achieve, whatever power he may attain and whatever deeds he may do, his life will remain way-less, so long as he does not face the Voice. Adam faces the Voice, perceives his enmeshment, and avows: "I hid myself"; this is the beginning of man's way. The decisive heart-searching is the beginning of the way in man's life; it is, again and again, the beginning of a human way.

But heart-searching is decisive only if it leads to the way. For there is a sterile kind of heart-searching, which leads to nothing but self-torture, despair and still deeper enmeshment. When the Rabbi of Ger,* in expounding the Scriptures, came to the words which Jacob addresses to his servant: "When Esau my brother meets thee, and asks thee, saying, Whose art thou? and whither goest thou? and whose are these before thee?" he would say to his disciples: "Mark well how similar Esau's questions are to the saying of our sages: 'Consider three things. Know whence you came, whither you are going, and to whom you will have to render accounts.' Be very careful, for great caution should be exercised by him who considers these three things: lest Esau ask in him. For Esau, too, may ask these questions and bring man into a state of gloom."

There is a demonic question, a spurious question, which apes God's question, the question of Truth. Its characteristic is that it does not stop at: "Where art thou?" but continues: "From where you have got to, there is no way out." This is the wrong kind of heart-searching, which does not prompt man to

* Góra Kalwarya near Warsaw.

turn or put him on the way, but, by representing turning as hopeless, drives him to a point where it appears to have become entirely impossible and lets him go on living only by demonic pride, the pride of perversity.

II. THE PARTICULAR WAY

Rabbi Baer of Radoshitz once said to his teacher, the "Seer" of Lublin: "Show me one general way to the service of God."

The zaddik replied: "It is impossible to tell men what way they should take. For one way to serve God is through learning, another through prayer, another through fasting, and still another through eating. Everyone should carefully observe what way his heart draws him to, and then choose this way with all his strength."

In the first place, this story tells us something about our relationship to such genuine service as was performed by others before us. We are to revere it and learn from it, but we are not to imitate it. The great and holy deeds done by others are examples for us, since they show, in a concrete manner, what greatness and holiness is, but they are not models which we should copy. However small our achievements may be in comparison with those of our forefathers, they have their real value in that we bring them about in our own way and by our own efforts.

The *maggid** of Zlotchov** was asked by a Hasid: "We are told: 'Everyone in Israel is in duty bound to say: When will my work approach the works of my fathers, Abraham, Isaac and Jacob?' How are we to understand this? How could we ever venture to think that we could do what our fathers did?"

The rabbi expounded: "Just as our fathers founded new ways of serving, each a new service according to his character: one the service of love, the other that of stern justice, the third that of beauty, so each of us in his own way shall devise something new in the light of teachings and of service, and do what has not yet been done."

Every person born into this world represents something new, something that never existed before, something original and unique. "It is the duty of every person in Israel to know and consider that he is unique in the world in his particular character

* preacher.
** town in Eastern Galicia.

and that there has never been anyone like him in the world, for if there had been someone like him, there would have been no need for him to be in the world. Every single man is a new thing in the world and is called upon to fulfill his particularity in this world. For verily: that this is not done is the reason why the coming of the Messiah is delayed." Every man's foremost task is the actualization of his unique, unprecedented and never-recurring potentialities, and not the repetition of something that another, and be it even the greatest, has already achieved.

The wise Rabbi Bunam once said in old age, when he had already grown blind: "I should not like to change places with our father Abraham! What good would it do God if Abraham became like blind Bunam, and blind Bunam became like Abraham? Rather than have this happen, I think I shall try to become a little more myself."

The same idea was expressed with even greater pregnancy by Rabbi Susya when he said, a short while before his death: "In the world to come I shall not be asked: 'Why were you not Moses?' I shall be asked: 'Why were you not Susya?' "

We are here confronted with a doctrine which is based on the fact that men are essentially unlike one another, and which therefore does not aim at making them alike. All men have access to God, but each man has a different access. Mankind's great chance lies precisely in the unlikeness of men, in the unlikeness of their qualities and inclinations. God's all-inclusiveness manifests itself in the infinite multiplicity of the ways that lead to him, each of which is open to one man. When some disciples of a deceased zaddik came to the Seer of Lublin and expressed surprise at the fact that his customs were different from those of their late master, the Seer exclaimed: "What sort of God would that be who has only one way in which he can be served!" But by the fact that each man, starting from his particular place and in a manner determined by his particular nature, is able to reach God, God can be reached by mankind, as such, through its multiple advance by all those different ways.

God does not say: "This way leads to me and that does not," but he says: "Whatever you do may be a way to me, provided you do it in such a manner that it leads you to me." But what it is that can and shall be done by just this person and no other can be revealed to him only in himself. In this matter, as I said before, it would only be misleading to study the achievements of another man and endeavor to equal him; for, in so doing, a man would miss precisely what he and he alone is called upon to do. The Baal-Shem said: "Every man should behave according to his 'rung.' If he does not, if he seizes the 'rung' of a fellow man and abandons his own, he will actualize neither the one nor the other." Thus, the way by which a man can reach God is revealed to him only through the knowledge of his own being, the knowledge of his essential quality and inclination. "Everyone has in him something precious that is in no one else." But this precious something in a man is revealed to him if he truly perceives his strongest feeling, his central wish, that in him which stirs his inmost being.

Of course, in many cases, a man knows this his strongest feeling only in the shape of a particular passion, of the "Evil Urge" which seeks to lead him astray. Naturally, a man's most powerful desire, in seeking satisfaction, rushes in the first instance at objects which lie across his path. It is necessary, therefore, that the power of even this feeling, of even this impulse, be diverted from the casual to the essential, and from the relative to the absolute. Thus a man finds his way.

A zaddik once said: "At the end of Ecclesiastes we read: 'At the end of the matter, the whole is heard: Fear God.' Whatever matter you follow to its end, there, at the end, you will hear one thing: 'Fear God', and this one thing is the whole. There is no thing in the world which does not point a way to the fear of God and to the service of God. Everything is commandment." By no means, however, can it be our true task, in the world into which we have been set, to turn away from the things and beings that we meet on our way and that attract our hearts; our task is precisely to get in touch, by hallowing our relationship with them, with what manifests itself in them as beauty, pleasure, enjoyment. Hasidism teaches that rejoicing in the world, if we hallow it with our whole being, leads to rejoicing in God.

One point in the tale of the Seer seems to contradict this, namely, that among the examples of "ways" we find not only eating but also fasting. But if we consider this in the general context of Hasidic teaching, it appears that though detachment from nature, abstinence from natural life, may, in the cases of some men, mean the necessary starting point of their "way" or, perhaps, a necessary act of self-isolation at certain crucial moments of existence, it may never mean the whole way. Some men must begin by fasting, and begin by it again and again, because it is peculiar to them that only by asceticism can they achieve liberation from their enslavement to the world, deepest heart-searching and ultimate communion with the Absolute. But never should asceticism gain mastery over a man's life. A man may only detach himself from nature in order to revert to it again and, in hallowed contact with it, find his way to God.

The Biblical passage which says of Abraham and the three visiting angels: "And he stood over them under the tree and they did eat" is interpreted by Rabbi Susya to the effect that man stands above the angels, because he knows something unknown to them, namely, that eating may be hallowed by the eater's intention. Through Abraham the angels, who were unaccustomed to eating, participated in the intention by which he dedicated it to God. Any natural act, if hallowed, leads to God, and nature needs man for what no angel can perform on it, namely, its hallowing.

III. RESOLUTION

A Hasid of the rabbi of Lublin once fasted from one Sabbath to the next. On Friday afternoon he began to suffer such cruel thirst that he thought he would die. He saw a well, went up to it, and prepared to drink. But instantly he realized that because of the one brief hour he had still to endure, he was about to destroy the work of the entire week. He did not drink and went away from the well. Then he was touched by a feeling of pride for having passed this difficult test. When he became aware of it, he said to himself, "Better I go and drink than let my heart fall prey to pride." He went back to the well, but just as he was going to bend down to draw water, he noticed that his thirst had disappeared. When the Sabbath had begun, he entered his teacher's house. "Patchwork!" the rabbi called to him, as he crossed the threshold.

When in my youth I heard this tale for the first time, I was struck by the harsh manner in which the master treats his zealous disciple. The latter makes his utmost efforts to perform a difficult feat of asceticism. He feels tempted to break off and overcomes the temptation, but his only reward, after all his trouble, is an expression of disapproval from his teacher. It is true that the disciple's first inhibition was due to the power of the body over the soul, a power which had still to be broken, but the second sprang from a truly noble motive: better to fail than, for the sake of succeeding, fall prey to pride. How can a man be scolded for such an inner struggle? Is this not asking too much of a man?

Long afterwards (but still as early as a quarter of a century ago), when I myself retold this tale from tradition, I understood that there was no question here of something being asked of a man. The zaddik of Lublin was no friend of asceticism, and the Hasid's fast was certainly not designed to please him, but to lift the Hasid's soul to a higher "rung"; the Seer himself had admitted that fasting could serve this purpose in the initial stage of a person's development and also later, at critical moments of his life. What the master—apparently after watching the progress of the venture with true understanding—says to the disciple means undoubtedly: "This is not the proper manner to attain a higher rung." He warns the disciple of something that perforce hinders him from achieving his purpose. What this is becomes clear enough. The object of the reproof is the advance and subsequent retreat; it is the wavering, shilly-shallying character of the man's doing that make it questionable. The opposite of "patchwork" is work "all of a piece." Now, how does one achieve work "all of a piece"? Only with a united soul.

Again we are troubled by the question whether this man is not being treated too harshly. As things are in this world, one man—"by nature" or "by grace," however one chooses to put it—has a unitary soul, a soul all of a piece, and accordingly performs unitary works, works all of a piece, because his soul, by being as it is, prompts and enables him to do so; another man has a divided, complicated, contradictory soul, and this, naturally, affects his doings: their inhibitions and disturbances originate in the inhibitions and disturbances of his soul; its restlessness is expressed in their restlessness. What else can a man so constituted do than try to overcome the temptations which approach him on the way to what is, at a given time, his goal? What else can he do than each time, in the middle of his doing, "pull himself together," as we say, that is, rally his vacillating soul, and again and again, having rallied it, re-concentrate it upon the goal—and moreover be ready, like the Hasid in the story when pride touches him, to sacrifice the goal in order to save the soul?

Only when, in the light of these questions, we subject our story to renewed scrutiny, do we apprehend the teaching implied in the Seer's criticism. It is the teaching that a man can unify his soul. The man with the divided, complicated, contradictory soul is not helpless: the core of his soul, the divine force in its depths, is capable of acting upon it, changing it, binding the conflicting forces together, amalgamating the diverging elements—is capable of unifying it. This unification must be accomplished *before* a man undertakes some unusual work. Only with a united soul will he be able so to do it that it becomes not patchwork but work all of a piece. The Seer thus reproaches the hasid with having embarked on his venture without first unifying his soul; unity of soul can never be achieved in the middle of the work. Nor should it be supposed that it can be brought about by asceticism; asceticism can purify, concentrate, but it cannot preserve its achievements intact until the attainment of the goal—it cannot protect the soul from its own contradiction.

One thing must of course not be lost sight of: unification of the soul is never final. Just as a soul most unitary from birth is sometimes beset by inner difficulties, thus even a soul most powerfully struggling for unity can never completely achieve it. But any work that I do with a united soul reacts upon my soul, acts in the direction of new and greater unification, leads me, though by all sorts of detours, to a *steadier* unity than was the preceding one. Thus man ultimately reaches a point where he can rely upon his soul, because its unity is now so great that it overcomes contradiction with effortless ease. Vigilance, of course, is necessary even then, but it is a relaxed vigilance.

On one of the days of the Hanukkah feast, Rabbi Nahum, the son of the rabbi of Rishyn,* entered the House of Study at a time when he was not expected and found his disciples playing checkers, as was the custom on those days. When they saw the zaddik they were embarrassed and stopped playing. But he gave them a kindly nod and asked: "Do you know the rules of the game of checkers?" And when they did not reply for shyness he himself gave the an-

* Ružyn (District of Kiev). Rabbi Israel of Rishyn was the founder of the famous "Dynasty of Sadagora."

swer: "I shall tell you the rules of the game of checkers. The first is that one must not make two moves at once. The second is that one may only move forward and not backward. And the third is that when one has reached the last row, one may move wherever one likes."

However, what is meant by unification of the soul would be thoroughly misunderstood if "soul" were taken to mean anything but: the whole man, body and spirit together. The soul is not really united, unless all bodily energies, all the limbs of the body, are united. The Baal-Shem interpreted the Biblical passage: "Whatsoever thy hand finds to do, do it with thy might" to the effect that the deeds one does should be done with every limb, i.e., even the whole of man's physical being should participate in it, no part of him should remain outside. A man who thus becomes a unit of body and spirit —he is the man whose work is all of a piece.

IV. BEGINNING WITH ONESELF

Once when Rabbi Yitzhak of Vorki was playing host to certain prominent men of Israel, they discussed the value to a household of an honest and efficient servant. They said that a good servant made for good management and cited Joseph at whose hands everything prospered. Rabbi Yitzhak objected. "I once thought that too," he said. "But then my teacher showed me that everything depends on the master of the house. You see, in my youth my wife gave me a great deal of trouble and, though I myself put up with her as best I could, I was sorry for the servants. So I went to my teacher, Rabbi David of Lelov, and asked him whether I should oppose my wife. All he said was: 'Why do you speak to me? Speak to yourself!' I thought over these words for quite a while before I understood them. But I did understand them when I recalled a certain saying of the Baal-Shem: 'There is thought, speech and action. Thought corresponds to one's wife, speech to one's children, and action to one's servants. Whoever straightens himself out in regard to all three will find that everything prospers at his hands.' Then I understood what my teacher had meant: everything depended on myself."

This story touches upon one of the deepest and most difficult problems of our life: the true origin of conflict between man and man.

Manifestations of conflict are usually explained either by the motives of which the quarreling parties are conscious as the occasion of their quarrel, and by the objective situations and processes which underlie these motives and in which both parties are involved; or, proceeding analytically, we try to explore the unconscious complexes to which these motives relate like mere symptoms of an illness to the organic disturbances themselves. Hasidic teaching coincides with this conception in that it, too, derives the problematics of external from that of internal life. But it differs in two essential points, one fundamental and one practical, the latter of which is even more important than the former.

The fundamental difference is that Hasidic teaching is not concerned with the exploration of particular psychical complications, but envisages man as a whole. This is, however, by no means a quantitative difference. For the Hasidic conception springs from the realization that the isolation of elements and partial processes from the whole hinders the comprehension of the whole, and that real transformation, real restoration, at first of the single person and subsequently of the relationship between him and his fellow men, can only be achieved by the comprehension of the whole as a whole. (Putting it paradoxically: the search for the center of gravity shifts it and thereby frustrates the whole attempt at overcoming the problematics involved.) This is not to say that there is no need to consider all the phenomena of the soul; but no one of them should be made so much the center of attention as if everything else could be derived from it; rather, they shall all be made starting points—not singly but in their vital connection.

The practical difference is that in Hasidism man is not treated as an object of examination but is called upon to "straighten himself out." At first, a man should himself realize that conflict-situations between himself and others are nothing but the effects of conflict-situations in his own soul; then he should try to overcome this inner conflict, so that afterwards he may go out to his fellow men and enter into new, transformed relationships with them.

Man naturally tries to avoid this decisive reversal—extremely repugnant to him in his accustomed relationship to the world—by referring him who thus appeals to him, or his own soul, if it is his soul that makes the appeal, to the fact that every conflict involves two parties and that, if he is expected to turn his attention from the external to his own internal conflict, his opponent should be expected to do the same. But just this perspective, in which a man sees himself only as an individual contrasted with other individuals, and not as a genuine person, whose transformation helps toward the transformation of the world, contains the fundamental error which Hasidic teaching denounces. The essential thing is to begin with oneself, and at this moment a man has nothing in the world to care about other than this beginning. Any other attitude would distract him from what he is about to begin, weaken his initiative, and thus frustrate the entire bold undertaking.

Rabbi Bunam taught:

"Our sages say: 'Seek peace in your own place.' You cannot find peace anywhere save in your own self. In the psalm we read: 'There is no peace in my bones because of my sin.' When a man has made peace within himself, he will be able to make peace in the whole world."

However, the story from which I started does not confine itself to pointing out the true origin of external conflicts, i.e., the internal conflict, in a general way. The quoted saying of the Baal-Shem states exactly in what the decisive inner conflict consists. It is the conflict between three principles in man's being and life, the principle of thought, the principle of speech, and the principle of action. The origin of all conflict between me and my fellow men is that I do not say what I mean, and that I do not do what I say. For this confuses and poisons, again and again and in increasing measure, the situation between myself and the other man, and I, in my internal disintegration, am no longer able to master it but, contrary to all my illusions, have become its slave. By our contradiction, our lie, we foster conflict-situations and give them power over us until they enslave us. From here, there is no way out but by the crucial realization: Everything depends on myself; and the crucial decision: I will straighten myself out.

But in order that a man may be capable of this great feat, he must first find his way from the casual, accessory elements of his existence to his own self; he must find his own self, not the trivial ego of the egotistic individual, but the deeper self of the person living in a relationship to the world. And that is also contrary to everything we are accustomed to.

I will close this chapter with an old jest as retold by a zaddik.

Rabbi Hanokh told this story:

There was once a man who was very stupid. When he got up in the morning it was so hard for him to find his clothes that at night he almost hesitated to go to bed for thinking of the trouble he would have on waking. One evening he finally made a great effort, took paper and pencil and as he undressed noted down exactly where he put everything he had on. The next morning, very well pleased with himself, he took the slip of paper in his hand and read: "cap"—there it was, he set it on his head; "pants"—there they lay, he got into them; and so it went until he was fully dressed. "That's all very well, but now where am I myself?" he asked in great consternation. "Where in the world am I?" He looked and looked, but it was a vain search; he could not find himself. "And that is how it is with us," said the rabbi.

V. NOT TO BE PREOCCUPIED WITH ONESELF

Rabbi Hayyim of Zans* had married his son to the daughter of Rabbi Eliezer. The day after the wedding he visited the father of the bride and said: "Now that we are related I feel close to you and can tell you what is eating at my heart. Look! My hair and beard have grown white, and I have not yet atoned!"

"O my friend," replied Rabbi Eliezer, "you are thinking only of yourself. How about forgetting yourself and thinking of the world?"

What is said here seems to contradict everything I have hitherto reported of the teachings of Hasidism. We have heard that everyone should search his own heart, choose his particular way, bring about the unity of his being, begin with him-

* Nowy Sacz in Western Galicia.

self; and now we are told that man should forget himself. But, if we examine this injunction more closely, we find that it is not only consistent with the others but fits into the whole as a necessary link, as a necessary stage, in its particular place. One need only ask one question: "What for?" What am I to choose my particular way for? What am I to unify my being for? The reply is: Not for my own sake. This is why the previous injunction was: to *begin* with oneself. To begin with oneself, but not to end with oneself; to start from oneself, but not to aim at oneself; to comprehend oneself, but not to be preoccupied with oneself.

We see a zaddik, a wise, pious, kindly man, reproach himself in his old age for not yet having performed the true turning. The reply given him is apparently prompted by the opinion that he greatly overrates his sins and greatly underrates the penance he has already done. But what Rabbi Eliezer says goes beyond this. He says, in quite a general sense: "Do not keep worrying about what you have done wrong, but apply the soul-power you are now wasting on self-reproach to such active relationship to the world as you are destined for. You should not be occupied with yourself but with the world."

First of all, we should properly understand what

is said here about turning. It is known that turning stands in the center of the Jewish conception of the way of man. Turning is capable of renewing a man from within and changing his position in God's world, so that he who turns is seen standing above the perfect zaddik who does not know the abyss of sin. But turning means here something much greater than repentance and acts of penance; it means that, by a reversal of his whole being, a man who had been lost in the maze of selfishness, where he had always set himself as his goal, finds a way to God, that is, a way to the fulfillment of the particular task for which he, this particular man, has been destined by God. Repentance can only be an incentive to such active reversal; he who goes on fretting himself with repentance, he who tortures himself with the idea that his acts of penance are not sufficient, withholds his best energies from the work of reversal. In a sermon on the Day of Atonement, the Rabbi of Ger warned against self-torture:

"He who has done ill and talks about it and thinks about it all the time does not cast the base thing he did out of his thoughts, and whatever one thinks therein one is, one's soul is wholly and utterly in what one thinks, and so he dwells in baseness. He will certainly not be able to turn, for his spirit will grow coarse and his heart stubborn, and in addition to this he may be overcome by gloom. What would you? Rake the muck this way, rake the muck that way—it will always be muck. Have I sinned, or have I not sinned—what does Heaven get out of it? In the time I am brooding over it I could be stringing pearls for the delight of Heaven. That is why it is written: 'Depart from evil and do good'—turn wholly away from evil, do not dwell upon it, and do good. You have done wrong? Then counteract it by doing right."

But the significance of our story goes beyond this. He who tortures himself incessantly with the idea that he has not yet sufficiently atoned is essentially concerned with the salvation of his soul, with his personal fate in eternity. By rejecting this aim, Hasidism merely draws a conclusion from the teachings of Judaism generally. One of the main points in which Christianity differs from Judaism is that it makes each man's salvation his highest aim. Judaism regards each man's soul as a serving member of God's Creation which, by man's work, is to become the Kingdom of God; thus no soul has its object in itself, in its own salvation. True, each is to know itself, purify itself, perfect itself, but not for its own sake—neither for the sake of its temporal happiness nor for that of its eternal bliss

—but for the sake of the work which it is destined to perform upon the world.

The pursuit of one's own salvation is here regarded merely as the sublimest form of self-intending. Self-intending is what Hasidism rejects most emphatically, and quite especially in the case of the man who has found and developed his own self. Rabbi Bunam said: "It is written: 'Now Korah took.' What did he take? He wanted to take himself—therefore, nothing he did could be of any worth." This is why Bunam contrasted the eternal Korah with the eternal Moses, the "humble" man, whose doings are not aimed at himself. Rabbi Bunam taught: "In every generation the soul of Moses and the soul of Korah return. But if once, in days to come, the soul of Korah is willing to subject itself to the soul of Moses, Korah will be redeemed."

Rabbi Bunam thus sees, as it were, the history of mankind on its road to redemption as a process involving two kinds of men, the proud who, if sometimes in the sublimest form, think of themselves, and the humble, who in all matters think of the world. Only when pride subjects itself to humility can it be redeemed; and only when it is redeemed can the world be redeemed.

After Rabbi Bunam's death, one of his disciples —the aforementioned Rabbi of Ger, from whose sermon on the Day of Atonement I quoted a few sentences—remarked: "Rabbi Bunam had the keys to all the firmaments. And why not? A man who does not think of himself is given all the keys."

The greatest of Rabbi Bunam's disciples, a truly tragic figure among the zaddikim, Rabbi Mendel of Kotzk, once said to his congregation: "What, after all, do I demand of you? Only three things: not to look furtively outside yourself, not to look furtively into others, and not to aim at yourselves." That is to say: firstly, everyone should preserve and hallow his own soul in its own particularity and in its own place and not envy the particularity and place of others; secondly, everyone should respect the secret in the soul of his fellow man and not, with brazen curiosity, intrude upon it and take advantage of it; and thirdly, everyone, in his relationship to the world, should be careful not to set himself as his aim.

VI. HERE WHERE ONE STANDS

Rabbi Bunam used to tell young men who came to him for the first time the story of Rabbi Eizik, son of Rabbi Yekel of Cracow. After many years of great poverty which had never shaken his faith in God, he dreamed someone bade him look for a treasure in Prague, under the bridge which leads to the king's palace. When the dream recurred a third time, Rabbi Eizik prepared for the journey and set out for Prague. But the bridge was guarded day and night and he did not dare to start digging. Nevertheless he went to the bridge every morning and kept walking around it until evening. Finally the captain of the guards, who had been watching him, asked in a kindly way whether he was looking for something or waiting for somebody. Rabbi Eizik told him of the dream which had brought him here from a faraway country. The captain laughed: "And so to please the dream, you poor fellow wore out your shoes to come here! As for having faith in dreams, if I had had it, I should have had to get going when a dream once told me to go to Cracow and dig for treasure under the stove in the room of a Jew—Eizik, son of Yekel, that was the name! Eizik, son of Yekel! I can just imagine what it would be like, how I should have to try every house over there, where one half of the Jews are named Eizik and the other Yekel!" And he laughed again. Rabbi Eizik bowed, traveled home, dug up the treasure from under the stove, and built the House of Prayer which is called "Reb Eizik Reb Yekel's Shul."

"Take this story to heart," Rabbi Bunam used to add, "and make what it says your own: There is something you cannot find anywhere in the world, not even at the zaddik's, and there is, nevertheless, a place where you can find it."

This, too, is a very old story, known from several popular literatures, but thoroughly reshaped by Hasidism. It has not merely—in a superficial sense—been transplanted into the Jewish sphere, it has been recast by the Hasidic melody in which it has been told; but even this is not decisive: the decisive change is that it has become, so to speak, transparent, and that a Hasidic truth is shining through its words. It has not had a "moral" appended to it, but the sage who retold it had at last discovered its true meaning and made it apparent.

There is something that can only be found in one place. It is a great treasure, which may be called the fulfillment of existence. The place where this treasure can be found is the place on which one stands.

Most of us achieve only at rare moments a clear realization of the fact that they have never tasted the fulfillment of existence, that their life does not participate in true, fulfilled existence, that, as it were, it passes true existence by. We nevertheless feel the deficiency at every moment, and in some measure strive to find—somewhere—what we are seeking. Somewhere, in some province of the world or of the mind, except where we stand, where we have been set—but it is there and nowhere else that the treasure can be found. The environment which I feel to be the natural one, the situation which has been assigned to me as my fate, the things that happen to me day after day, the things that claim me day after day—these contain my essential task and such fulfillment of existence as is open to me. It is said of a certain Talmudic master that the paths of heaven were as bright to him as the streets of his native town. Hasidism inverts the order: It is a greater thing if the streets of a man's native town are as bright to him as the paths of heaven. For it is here, where we stand, that we should try to make shine the light of the hidden divine life.

If we had power over the ends of the earth, it would not give us that fulfillment of existence which a quiet devoted relationship to nearby life can give us. If we knew the secrets of the upper worlds, they would not allow us so much actual participation in true existence as we can achieve by performing, with holy intent, a task belonging to our daily duties. Our treasure is hidden beneath the hearth of our own home.

The Baal-Shem teaches that no encounter with a being or a thing in the course of our life lacks a hidden significance. The people we live with or meet with, the animals that help us with our farm work, the soil we till, the materials we shape, the tools we use, they all contain a mysterious spiritual substance which depends on us for helping it toward its pure form, its perfection. If we neglect this spiritual substance sent across our path, if we think only in terms of momentary purposes, without developing a genuine relationship to the beings and things in whose life we ought to take part, as they in ours, then we shall ourselves we debarred from true, fulfilled existence. It is my conviction that this doctrine is essentially true. The highest culture of the soul remains basically arid and barren unless, day by day, waters of life pour forth into the soul from those little encounters to which we give their due; the most formidable power is intrinsically powerlessness unless it maintains a secret covenant with these contacts, both humble and helpful, with strange, and yet near, being.

Some religions do not regard our sojourn on earth as true life. They either teach that everything appearing to us here is mere appearance, behind which we should penetrate, or that it is only a forecourt of the true world, a forecourt which we should cross without paying much attention to it. Judaism, on the contrary, teaches that what a man does now and here with holy intent is no less important, no less true—being a terrestrial indeed, but none the less factual, link with divine being—than the life in the world to come. This doctrine has found its fullest expression in Hasidism.

Rabbi Hanokh said: "The other nations too believe that there are two worlds. They too say: 'In the other world.' The difference is this: They think that the two are separate and severed, but Israel professes that the two worlds are essentially one and shall in fact become one."

In their true essence, the two worlds are one.

They only have, as it were, moved apart. But they shall again become one, as they are in their true essence. Man was created for the purpose of unifying the two worlds. He contributes toward this unity by holy living, in relationship to the world in which he has been set, at the place on which he stands.

Once they told Rabbi Pinhas of the great misery among the needy. He listened, sunk in grief. Then he raised his head. "Let us draw God into the world," he cried, "and all need will be stilled."

But is this possible, to draw God into the world? Is this not an arrogant, presumptuous idea? How dare the lowly worm touch upon a matter which depends entirely on God's grace: how much of Himself He will vouchsafe to His creation?

Here again, Jewish doctrine is opposed to that of other religions, and again it is in Hasidism that it has found its fullest expression. God's grace consists precisely in this, that He wants to let Himself be won by man, that He places Himself, so to speak, into man's hands. God wants to come to His world, but He wants to come to it through man. This is the mystery of our existence, the superhuman chance of mankind.

"Where is the dwelling of God?"

This was the question with which the Rabbi of

Kotzk surprised a number of learned men who happened to be visiting him.

They laughed at him: "What a thing to ask! Is not the whole world full of His glory?"

Then he answered his own question:

"God dwells wherever man lets Him in."

This is the ultimate purpose: to let God in. But we can let Him in only where we really stand, where we live, where we live a true life. If we maintain holy intercourse with the little world entrusted to us, if we help the holy spiritual substance to accomplish itself in that section of Creation in which we are living, then we are establishing, in this our place, a dwelling for the Divine Presence.

BOOK V

THE BAAL-SHEM-TOV'S INSTRUCTION IN INTERCOURSE WITH GOD

INTRODUCTION

This text (completed many years ago) consists of a selection of fragments, transmitted as citations in books of disciples and disciples' disciples, from the speech of a man who himself wrote no book.

This man is one of the leading figures in the spiritual history of Judaism, the leader of that powerful Jewish movement called *Hasidut*—a word that can be translated into English still far less than the Latin *pietas* that corresponds to it; its meaning might most easily be rendered through a verbal paraphrase: to love the world in God. Furthermore, this man is one of the central figures in the religious history of the eighteenth century, the greater counterpart of Zinzendorf (in the same year as whom he was probably born and in the same died, and of whom he certainly knew nothing). Through both the rediscovery of "standing over against," the real mutuality, was accomplished—the German discovered it in the detachment of feelings, the Polish Jew in the inclusion of the whole of world life. (The German philosophical sequel ended with the young Schleiermacher, the Jewish has begun with the work of Hermann Cohen's old age.)

In a time that has learned to give attention to the contribution of Judaism to human work, the Baal-Shem will probably be extolled as the founder of a realistic and active mysticism, i.e., a mysticism for which the world is not an illusion, from which man must turn away in order to reach true being, but the reality between God and him in which reciprocity manifests itself, the subject of the message of creation to him, the subject of his answering service of creation, destined to be redeemed through the meeting of divine and human need; a mysticism, hence, without the intermixture of principles and without the weakening of the lived multiplicity of all for the sake of a unity of all that is to be experienced (*Yihud*, *unio*, means not the unification of the soul with God, but unification of God with His glory that dwells in the world). A "mysticism" that may be called such because it preserves the immediacy of the relation, guards the concreteness of the absolute and demands the involvement of the whole being; one can, to be sure, also call it religion for just the same reason. Its true English name is perhaps: presentness.

But if one really wishes to receive the words of the Baal-Shem assembled in this text, one will do well to forget all that one knows of history and all that one imagines one knows of mysticism and, while reading listen to a human voice that speaks today, here, to those who today and here read.

OF KNOWLEDGE

Would that they had forsaken me, says God, and kept my teaching!

That is to be explained thus:

The ultimate apprehension of knowing is that we cannot know. But there are two types of not knowing. The one is the immediate: there one does not even begin to search and to know because it is indeed impossible to know. But another man searches and seeks until he knows that one cannot know. And the difference between the two—to whom can they be compared? To two who wish to get to know the king. The one enters all the rooms of the king, he rejoices in the king's treasury and halls of splendor, and then he learns that he cannot come to know the king. The other says to himself: Since it is not possible to come to know the king, we shall not enter at all but resign ourselves to not knowing.

From this is to be understood what that word of God's signifies: They have forsaken me—that is, they have abandoned knowing me because it is not possible; but would they had forsaken me then out of searching and knowing through keeping my teaching!

Why do we say: "Our God and God of our fathers"?

There are two kinds of men who believe in God. The one believes because it is handed down to him by his fathers; and his belief is strong. The other has come to his belief through searching. And this is the difference between them: the superiority of the first lies in the fact that his faith cannot be shattered no matter how many arguments one may bring against it, for his faith is firm because he has taken it over from his fathers; but it has a defect: that his faith is only a human command, learned without meaning and understanding. The superiority of the second lies in the fact that because he has found God through searching, he has arrived at his own faith; but for him too there remains a defect: that it is easy to shake his faith through proof to the contrary. To him who unites both, however, none is superior. Therefore we say: "Our God," because of our searching, and "God of our fathers," for the sake of our tradition.

And thus also it is explained that we say: "God of Abraham, God of Isaac, and God of Jacob," but we do not say: "God of Abraham, Isaac, and Jacob"—by this is said: Isaac and Jacob could not rest on Abraham's tradition alone, but themselves sought the divine.

OF FERVOR AND OF WORK

He takes unto himself the quality of fervor.[1]* He arises from sleep with fervor, for he is hallowed and become another man and is worthy to create and is become like the Holy One, blessed be He, when He created His world.

All that you are able to do, do it with your strength! That is, bind the deed to the strength of thought. As it is told of Enoch, that he was a cobbler and with every stitch of his awl, which sewed the upper leather to the sole, bound the holy God with the indwelling Glory.[2]

Our sages say: "Micah came and based it on three things"[3]; that is, he fortified the law through the three pillars on which the world rests: 'Do

* The numerals in this section refer to the explanatory notes at the end of Book V.

justly,' that is righteousness, 'and love mercy,' that is good deeds, 'and walk humbly with thy God,' that is the middle pillar, the order of truth: that your mouth and your heart be one and be directed to no distracting aim, to none of the evil powers that are called 'the dead.' " Therefore our sages say: "Walk humbly, that is funeral procession and receiving the bride"; first the dead, the evil powers, are led forth, and then the bride enters: for he who unites his mouth and his heart, he unites the bridegroom with the bride—the Holy God with the Indwelling Glory.

Through a perverted humility one can remove himself from the service of God: if through self-abasement he does not believe that man through praying and teaching brings down the fullness over all worlds and even the angels nourish themselves from his learning and praying. If he believed in this, how he would then serve God in greater fear and joy, and take care with every movement and every word to speak and to act in the right way!

Man should think of himself as a ladder, placed upon the earth and touching heaven with its head, and all his gestures and affairs and speaking leave traces in the higher world.

OF THE HOLY SPARKS AND THEIR REDEMPTION

The holy sparks that fell when God built and destroyed worlds,[4] man shall raise and purify upward from stone to plant, from plant to animal, from animal to speaking being, purify the holy sparks that are imprisoned in the world of shells. That is the basic meaning of the service of each one in Israel.

It is known that each spark that dwells in a stone or plant or another creature has a complete figure with the full number of limbs and sinews and, when it dwells in the stone or plant, it is in prison, cannot stretch out its hands and feet and cannot speak, but its head lies on its knees. And who with the good strength of his spirit is able to raise the holy spark from stone to plant, from plant to animal, from animal to speaking being, he leads it into freedom, and no setting free of captives is greater than this. It is as when a king's son is rescued from captivity and brought to his father.

All that man has, his servant, his animals, his tools, all conceal sparks that belong to the roots of his soul and wish to be raised by him to their origin.

All things of this world that belong to him desire with all their might to draw near him in order that the sparks of holiness that are in them should be raised by him.

Man eats them, man drinks them, man uses them; these are the sparks that dwell in the things. Therefore, one should have mercy on his tools and all his possessions for the sake of the sparks that are in them; one should have mercy on the holy sparks.

Take care that all that you do for God's sake be itself service of God. Thus eating: do not say that the intention of eating shall be that you gain strength for the service of God. This is also a intention, of course; but the true perfection only exists where the deed itself happens to heaven, that is where the holy sparks are raised.

In all that is in the world dwell holy sparks, no thing is empty of them. In the actions of men also, indeed even in the sins that a man does, dwell holy sparks[5] of the glory of God. And what is it that the sparks await that dwell in the sins? It is the turning. In the hour where you turn on account of sin, you raise to the higher world the sparks that were in it.

HOW ONE SHOULD SERVE

Man should serve God with his whole strength, for all is needed. For God wills that one serve Him in all ways.

And this means: when one at times goes about and talks with people, and at that time he cannot learn, then he shall cleave to God and unite with his soul the names of God;[6] and when one sets out on a trip and cannot then pray according to his custom, then he shall serve God in other ways. And he should not grieve himself over it; for God wills that one serve Him in all ways, at times in this, at other times in that way, and for this reason He had appointed that he should go on a trip or talk with people, in order that he may also perform this service.

How One Should Serve

This is the mystery of the oneness of God, that at whatever place I, a tiny bit, lay hold of it, I lay hold of the whole. And since the teaching and all commandments are radiations of His being, so he who fulfills a command in love to its very ground, and in this command lays hold of a tiny bit of the oneness of God, holds the whole in his hand as though he had fulfilled all.

When we do not believe[7] that God renews each day the work of creation, then our prayer and fulfillment of the commands becomes old and routine and bored. As it says in the Psalm, "Do not cast me off when I am old," that is, do not let my world become old. And in Lamentations it says, "New each morning, great is Thy faithfulness"—that the world becomes new for us each morning, that is Thy great faithfulness.

OF DISTANCE AND NEARNESS

At times man must realize that there are infinitely many firmaments and spheres, and he stands on a speck of the little earth, but the whole of the universe is as nothing before God who is the boundless and who limited Himself and set a place in Himself[8] in which to create the world. And although man can grasp this with his insight, he cannot ascend to the higher worlds; and this is what is written: "Appears out of the distance with the Lord"—he beholds God out of the distance. But if he serves God with all his might, then he encompasses great power within himself and exalts himself in his spirit and at once breaks through all firmaments and ascends over angels and heavenly cycles and seraphim and thrones: and that is the perfect service.

He who does the right or applies himself to the teaching in the fervor of cleaving to God, he makes his body the throne of the life-soul and the life-soul the throne of the heart and the heart the throne of the spirit and the spirit the throne of the light of the indwelling glory, and he sits in the midst of the light and trembles and rejoices. As a token of this,[9] heaven appears at each place as a hemisphere.

"Noah went with God." Noah adhered so closely to God that each step that he took seemed to be guided by God as though God stood over against him and set his feet right and led him as a father who teaches his little son to walk. Therefore, when the Father withdrew from him, Noah knew: "That is in order that I might learn to walk."

OF SECRECY

Man may enjoy all good things and mortify himself with bliss. He may look wherever he will and not stray beyond his circle of four ells, for in all things he preserves the secret name of God. He may stand unmoving in prayer so that none marks his service, but secretly his spirit burns, and he shouts in the silence.

At times a man rests on his bed, and it appears to his family as though he were asleep, but he spends this hour in solitude with his Creator, blessed be He. That is a high rung, that he beholds the Creator at all times with the eye of his insight, as he sees another man. And consider this: if you persevere in a pure thought, then the Creator also looks at you, as a man looks at you.

Of Secrecy

There are two kinds of love. One man loves the acts and speech of his clever son and boasts to his friends that he does and says clever things; the other loves his son himself whatever he may say and do. So it is with the love of God for man. When a proven man fulfills commands and good works in great wisdom, then God loves his deed and is present to all his doings, and thus the externals of the world are bound to God. But when the proven man himself adheres to God, then God loves him himself even though he does not accomplish his works in wisdom, rather walks in great simplicity and cleaves to God; for just this reason God loves him. And thus the inwardness of the world is raised to God.

A PARABLE OF PRAYER

Prayer is a coupling with the Glory of God. Therefore man should move himself up and down at the beginning of prayer, but then he can stand unmoved and cleave to God in a great cleaving. And because he moves, he can attain to a great awakening so that he must reflect: Why do I move up and down? Certainly, because the Glory of God stands over against me. And over this he enters into a great rapture.

In my flesh,"[10] says Job, "I shall see God."

As in bodily coupling, only he can beget who uses a living limb with longing and joy, so in the spiritual coupling, that is, with the speaker of the teaching and of the prayer, it is he who performs them with living limb in joy and bliss who begets.

A Parable of Prayer

As the bride at the wedding is clothed and adorned with all kinds of garments, but when the nuptials themselves are to take place, the garments are taken from her in order that the bodies can come close to each other, so it says too: "Out of my flesh shall I see God," for prayer is the bride who at first is adorned with many garments, but then, when her friend embraces her, all clothing is taken from her.

OF TRUE INTENTION

It is said,[11] "One does not pray otherwise than out of a heaviness of the head." That is to be understood thus: Do not pray for a thing that you lack, for your prayer will not be accepted. Rather when you wish to pray, pray because of the heaviness that is in the head of the world.[12] For the want of the thing that you lack is in the indwelling Glory. For man is a part of God, and the want that is in the part is in the whole, and the whole suffers the want of the part. Therefore let your prayer be directed to the want of the whole.

Prayer is a high need. For man knows of his want that it comes from a higher one, and he prays that the wants of the Glory be satisfied. And then his own wants will be satisfied at the same time.

Man should not think about the satisfaction either of the higher or the lower that he be not like him who cuts off the eternal plants[13] and causes separation. Rather he does all for the sake of the want of the Glory, and all will be resolved of itself, and his own suffering too will be stilled out of the stilling of the higher roots. For all, above and below, is one unity.

Pray continually for God's Glory that it may be redeemed from its exile.[14]

Man should unite all things of the world with all his thinking, speaking, doing, toward God in truth and simplicity. For no thing of the world is set outside the unity of God. But he who does a thing otherwise than toward God separates it from Him.

OF THE MIGHT OF WORDS

When you speak, bear in mind the mystery of the voice and of the word and speak in fear and love and reflect that the world of the word[15] speaks out of your mouth. Then you will uplift the word.

Reflect that you are only a vessel, that your thought and your word are worlds that expand: the world of the word, that is the indwelling Glory, longs in this speech for something of the world of thought. And when you have drawn the light of God into your thinking and your word, then let this be your prayer, that the fullness which blesses overflow out of the world of thought over the world of the word. Then you too will receive what you need. Therefore it says, "Let us find you in our prayers!" In our prayers themselves God lets Himself be found.

He who in his prayer employs all the arts of intention[16] that he knows effects only just what he knows. But he who speaks the word with great binding to God, for him there enters of itself into that world the totality of intention. For each letter is a complete world, and he who speaks the word with great binding awakens those higher worlds and does a great work.

In each letter there are the three: world, soul, and divinity. They join and unite with one another. And then the letters unite and join themselves, and they become the word. They unite themselves in the divine in genuine unity. And man shall enclose his soul in each of the three: then all will unite themselves to one, and there will be great rapture without limit.

OF DEVOTION

Man should reflect before prayer that he is ready to die in this prayer for the sake of its intention.

Know that each word is a complete figure, and it is necessary to be in it with your whole strength, for if there is not enough strength brought to it, then it is like the defect in a limb.

It is a great mercy of God that man lives after prayer. For according to the way of nature, he must die because all his strength is in it; for he has devoted his strength in prayer for the sake of the great intention.

OF BINDING

When I fix my thoughts on the Creator, I let my mouth speak what it will, for the words are bound to the higher roots.

When man bears ever new fire to the altar of his soul, the sparks of the indwelling Glory that are in him are inflamed, and they speak the words with his mouth so that it seems as if he remained silent and the words came out of his mouth of themselves.

OF DISTRACTING THOUGHTS

In the hour of teaching and of prayer there is no curtain separating man and his God. Even when many alien thoughts ascend in you, they are garments and covers behind which the Holy One, blessed be He, conceals Himself, and when you know about this, there is no longer any concealment.

When man prays and an alien thought comes to him, then the power of the shells[17] rides on the word; for the thought rides on the word.

In all thoughts of man the reality of God conceals itself. And each thought is a complete figure. And when in the thinking of man at the time of his prayer an evil or an alien thought arises, it comes to him in order that he may redeem it and let it ascend. But he who does not believe in this does not truly take on himself the yoke of the kingdom of heaven.

And Jacob awoke from his sleep and spoke: 'Truly, HE is present in this place, and I knew it not.' And he shuddered and said: 'How dreadful is this place!' "

"HE is present in this place"—that means: Where the living assemble, there is God's name. Thus in all alien and evil thoughts, which are the war-bands of life and robbers and the power of the shells of evil, there also dwell holy sparks of Glory that fell down in the primordial time when the vessels of creation broke in pieces.

"And he shuddered and said: 'How dreadful is this place!' " Dread and trembling overcame him because he suffered the pain of the Glory and its downfall to the power of the shells of evil. Thereby a unification of the shudderer with what inspired the shudder took place, and the shells broke asunder.

The alien thoughts come to man in the midst of his prayer out of the mystery of the breaking in pieces of the primal vessels because men shall purify them each day, and they come to him as to their redemption. And the alien thoughts of today are not like those of tomorrow.

Man binds his impulses to God. When an evil love overcomes him, he directs his love to God alone and all his striving merges in this love. And when anger, that is, an evil fear which derives from the quality of power, takes possession of him, then he masters his impulse and makes out of just this quality a carriage for God.

OF GOOD AND EVIL

The indwelling Glory prevails from above to below unto the rim of all rungs. That is the mystery of the word, "And you animate them all." Even when man does a sin, then too the Glory is clothed in it, for without it he would not have the strength to move a limb. And this is the exile of God's Glory.

In the story of creation it says, "Indeed, it was very good." But in the exhortation of Moses it says, "See, I have placed before you this day life and good, death and evil." From where has evil come?

Evil too is good, it is the lowest rung of perfect goodness. If one does good, then evil too becomes good; but if one sins, then it becomes really evil.

The indwelling Glory embraces all worlds, all creatures, good and evil. And it is the true unity. How can it then bear in itself the opposites of good and evil? But in truth there is no opposite, for the evil is the throne of the good.

As the Glory embraces all worlds, good and evil, so were they enclosed in Moses.

When God called to Moses the first time, he did not answer, "Here am I," because he was lost in astonishment: How then can the unification take place? For when God revealed Himself in the thorn bush, that is, in evil, as in the lowest rung, all the fountains of fire opened themselves, from the highest unto the depths—but the thorn bush did not burn up, the evil was not consumed: how could that happen? Then God called a second time: "Moses!"—then the lowest rung bound itself to the highest in Moses himself,[18] and he said, "Here am I."

OF PRIDE AND HUMILITY

Do not say in your heart that you are greater than your fellow because you serve God with fervor. You are nothing other than a creature who was created for the service of God. And in what are you more to be esteemed than a worm? Does he not then serve the Creator with his whole insight and strength!

When you talk with people, do not examine whether their thoughts constantly cleave to God. The examining soul suffers injury.

If it should happen to you that you see a sin or hear of one, seek your share in this sin and strive to set yourself to rights. Then even that evil man too will turn. You must only embrace him in your turning according to the meaning of the unity, for all are one man.

These are the words that Moses said to all Israel beyond the Jordan in the wilderness."

Many a man who thinks he has God knows nothing of Him. To many who believe they long for Him out of the distance, He is near. But you ought always to feel that you stand on the shore of the Jordan and have not yet entered the Land. And if you have already fulfilled all kinds of commandments, know still that you have done nothing.

There are two extreme types among men. The one is a wholly evil man who knows his Lord and intends to rebel against him. The other in his delusion considers himself a wholly righteous man. In truth, however, whether he incessantly learns and prays and mortifies himself, he exerts himself in vain, for he does not have the faithfulness. And this is the difference between them: For the wholly evil man there exists a cure for his defect—when the turning awakens in him and he turns with his whole heart to God and entreats Him to show him the way where the light dwells. But the other, who is incapable of seeing the greatness of the Creator and the real service of Him, because he is righteous in his own eyes—how can he turn?

Pride is more serious than all sin. For to all sinning applies God's word about Himself: "Who dwells in the midst of their uncleanness." But of the proud man God says, as our sages teach, "I and he cannot dwell together in the world."

Even the followers of Abraham knew pride, even the followers of Balaam knew humility. But the former had the right sort of pride; they lifted their hearts and dared to accomplish great things on behalf of God. And the latter had the wrong humility; they debased their hearts and did not trust themselves to fulfill the commandment: Depart from evil and do good; that is, make out of the evil good.

OF THE TWOFOLD MOVEMENT

If the power of procreation first stirs in the woman, then a male child is born. And the masculine[19] is the symbol of mercy.

If the movement first awakens from below, then the divine quality of mercy prevails.

Of it it says too, "I awaken the dawn."

And indeed it is written of the day of Atonement: "On this day you are covered over"—even if they are not awakened to it of themselves, atonement is awakened from above, "to purify yourself: from all your sins." But now follows the word of proper salvation: "Before God purify yourself"—before God stirs you, you shall stir yourself.

And thus Rabbi Akiba says: "Heal yourself, Israel! Before whom do you purify yourselves and who is it that purifies you? Your Father in Heaven." The beginning is up to you. For if the power of procreation first stirs in the woman, a male child is born.

EXPLANATORY NOTES

1—"the quality of fervor"

What is meant is the divine attribute of "readiness," the power to effect that is accorded to man who is created in the image of God. Man awakens every morning before *the fall into sin, in the pure state of likeness to God, and on each morning it is up to him, as it was in the primal time, whether he will realize or bring to naught what has been accorded to him.*

2—"bound the Holy God with the indwelling Glory"

The man who establishes unity in himself between the realm of thought and the realm of deed, works on the unification between the realm of thought and the realm of deed, that is, between God and His creation in which he allows His Shekina ("indwelling"), His Glory, to dwell. In fulfilling every commandment, man shall say: "I do this in order to unite the Holy One, blessed be He, with His Shekina." But it would mean a distortion of the teaching to understand this unification as taking place "in" God. That the Shekina associates itself with creation may not be grasped as a division within God; no immanence, even so unconditional a one as this, can mean a diminution of the perfection of His transcendence. The suspended paradox of the overlapping influence of the human essential deed has its truth in the inwardness of now and here; it would become nonsense if the conception of a change in the being of God were combined with it.

3—"Micah came and based it on three things"

The Talmud (Makkot 23f.) lets the six hundred and thirteen commandments and prohibitions that Moses received on Mount Sinai be reduced by David to eleven, by Isaiah to six, by Micah (6:8) to three and by Habakkuk to one single one that indeed no longer has the ring of a command but of a promise: "The proven man shall live through his trust." *Micah's phrase, "walk humbly" is explained by the Talmud passage as the pious prac-*

tices of accompanying the bride into the bridal chamber and the dead to the "house of life," but to the Baal-Shem this phrase again becomes the symbol of an essential act.

4—"when God built and destroyed worlds"

According to the Midrash (Bereshit Rabba to Genesis 1:5 and 1:31) God created and cast away many worlds before He created this one; it is to this that the verse refers, "Then God saw all that He had made: indeed, it was very good." But only the Kabbala gives this pre-creation a greater meaning than that of a gradual perfecting. With "the breaking to pieces of the vessels," i.e., the chaotic pre-worlds that could not bear the divine fullness, the "holy sparks" have fallen into the "shells," the separating, hindering, demonic enclosures that alone are "evil." But they fell in order to be raised: for the sake of man's working on redemption those worlds existed and ceased to be.

5—"even in the sins that a man does dwell holy sparks"

The chosen disciple of the Baal-Shem, the "Great Maggid," said, "The turning lies hidden in sin as oil in the olive."

6—"unite the names of God"

The "names" are God's powers of manifestation, his "measures" or qualities (middot). *Of these the name* Elohim *designates the quality of power and judgment; the not-to-be-pronounced name represented by the consonants YHVH designates the quality of grace and mercy; the former signifies the limitation of the divine to "nature," the infinite wonder to law, the incomprehensible light to the comprehensible; the latter the becoming present to the creature of Being itself that is nothing other than grace, but that enters into the restriction because all that is created perishes before the divine fullness of grace. The man who with his soul unites the two names prepares within himself a place for unification and works for redemption, which is the completed unification: as the state in which the limitation by virtue of which the world exists is not abolished; but over it, without injuring it, the fullness of grace shines forth.*

7—"when we do not believe"

The daily prayer of the Jew confesses this belief in the words: "Who in His goodness each day continually renews the work of the beginning."

8—"and set a place in Himself"

This is not to be understood as though God were "infinite" and set finitude in Himself. God is not infinite, but "boundless." "Infinite" space and "infinite time" are only bounds with which He Himself limits Himself in creating. The Great Maggid answered the childlike question why God had not created the world "earlier" with the statement that time too has been created and thus no "earlier" existed. He thus expressed this truth: God does not create "in time," He creates time; and even so He creates space. But he who serves God with all his might breaks through this "firmament" and stands in the spaceless nearness *which, even though it is no less a standing over against than the distance, is raised above the bounds.*

9—"as a token of this"

As the sky overarches each piece of earth as though it were there alone and belonged to it, so the divine light does not appear in a beyond, but over every completed here and now.

10—"In my flesh"

The meaning of this phrase from Job (19:20) is in dispute; it says literally "from my flesh" but that can either mean: "from out of my flesh, in my flesh," or: "out of my flesh, without my flesh." In the second and third sayings of this section there follow both interpretations, one after the other, and here they no longer contend with each other; for "in the flesh" points to the wholeness *of man demanded for real life and "out of the flesh" to the* inwardness *of the word that enters into real life, and both belong together.*

11—"It is said"

The Mishna passage (Berachot V) means that bowing must precede prayer; therefore, it says further, "pious men" before they pray spend an hour in wordless meditation in order to direct their heart to their heavenly Father. This intention (kavana), *this "directing" of the collected human being to God, is the basic practical motif of Hasidic teaching. The Kabbala succumbed ever again to the danger of turning intention into a kind of magic, of narrowing it to a kind of mystical-technical preoccupation with the mysteries of the divine names—a danger that can be compared with the technicizing of the cult of sacrifice (which was probably also joined with magical and primitive-mystical conceptions); and as, in opposition to this technicizing, the prophets summoned men to or back to true in-*

tention of the whole man, so now the founder of Hasidut.

12—"because of the heaviness that is in the head of the world"

Because of the suffering of God in the world. The Shekina, that dwells in the world, is also the God who suffers for the world.

13—"like him who cuts off the eternal plants"

This expression is used in the Talmud (Haggiga 14b) of the great heretic Elisha ben Abuya, called Acher ("the other"). It wishes to say that he taught a dualism that tears asunder the divine self-being and the rule of the world, places the latter under an independent power and thus robs the Holy One of his working, the reality of his hallowing.

14—"that it may be redeemed from its exile"

The Shekina suffers directly the fall of the world, of man, of the people of Israel, and it follows the creature into the dark province that those who have fallen enter, into exile.

15—"the world of the word"

The Shekina is the Word that has entered into creation; the God who rules over His creation, from whom the Word goes forth and to whom it returns home, is "the thought." This divine double aspect of the One corresponds to that of thought and word in man.

16—"arts of intention"

The Kabbalistic technique of kavana, *in particular the displacing, rendering independent, and combining of the letters of the names of God and absorption in them.*

17—"the power of the shells"

The powers of evil are called klipot, *shells, in the Kabbala. Evil is not a substance that stands in opposition to the good, but only its veil and hindrance. The good is held captive in the shells; when it holds its ground and proves true, the shells dissolve and ascend in them.*

18—"bound itself to the highest in Moses himself"

Man, to whom God does not reveal Himself in harmony but in extended oppositeness of principles, is given over to confusion and must despair of the salvation of the world so long as he stares inactive into the burning contradiction. Only when the unification takes place in his own soul, which overcomes the same oppositeness, can he reply to the divine revelation, and replying he experiences the unity of being, the salvation of the world.

19—"the masculine"

Of the two "measures" or fundamental qualities of God, the quality of mercy, of the fullness of grace, and that of judgment, of limitation, the former is conceived of as masculine, the latter as feminine. But, too, the relationship between God and His world appears in the image of marriage. In order that "a male child be born," in order that grace accomplish its work of redeeming the world, an effecting must proceed from the world itself. The world, to be sure, can only begin, nothing more; but just this is allotted to it, for this it was created—"in the beginning," that is expounded: for the sake of its beginning.

LOVE OF GOD AND LOVE OF NEIGHBOR

The age-old controversy between religion and ethics which has continued into our days has two basic forms according to which side takes the lead. The advance of ethics generally takes place under the sign of the question: heteronomy or autonomy? The advance of religion generally has as its goal to establish its primacy. A just decision between the two seems to me possible, as so often, only by acknowledging both right and both wrong. In so doing, naturally, we must precisely delimit from each other the sphere of right and the sphere of wrong.

Shall one, asks ethics, do the good because the gods command it or because it is the good? In contrast, religion on its side poses the question: Shall one make the good primary at all, or that which

God wills of one? The first question obviously distinguishes merely between two motives for the same moral action and wants to know which is the right one. The second question, in contrast, distinguishes essentially between two kinds of actions and wants to know which is superior. It is of fundamental importance to religion, though, that the motive be "for God's sake." In other words, the first question leaves undecided whether, according to the content of actions, a complete harmony between religion and ethics might not be possible; the second has in view a possible conflict between the two and wishes to insure pre-eminence for the first in the case of conflict. Both questions proceed, in the final analysis, from a false conception both of religion and of ethics.

Man either believes in a commanding and claiming God or he does not believe in such a God (this distinction, and not that between "believers" and "unbelievers," is the decisive one for us here). For him who does not believe thus, ethics, of course, is simply right: he shall and can do the good only because it is the good. It is simply right when it places the man who is good but who does not believe in a commanding and claiming God in opposition to the religious position: of course, good actions are not less good when they are performed out of one's own insight, one's own impulses, or one's own conscience. Beyond this point, however, begins the problematic in the existence of this man. If he is a religious man, then no connection in the strict sense exists between his isolated ethical and his isolated religious life; they stand under different laws, his life has no elemental wholeness.

It is otherwise with the non-religious man: he can not merely be admirable in every other respect, he can even possess the wholeness in his personal life that the other lacks; but he does not have real contact with the wholeness of being, that is, his life as such is isolated over against the wholeness of being. This is, to be sure, a point that only the religious, not the non-religious man, can understand: here is the boundary of the conceptual understanding between the two, and the non-religious man is still at liberty to reject this criticism as illusionary. But in both cases ethics with its postulate of autonomy is in the right.

What then if we speak of the man who believes in a commanding and claiming God? Let us take first of all a type that is especially significant for our age. This is the man who does not have the faith that he knows with assurance through a tradition what God commands him to do in his life. Instead he regards the traditional revelation as a fusion of the divine and the human within which the human share increases in the course of its being handed down while the divine only directly reveals itself as the divine in occasional hours of personal illumination and only in certain biographical situations—this man quite literally lives in "fear and trembling." In principle, to be sure, no problem of autonomy and heteronomy exists for him, for he knows that, if he were in full harmony with his God, then just that which is God's will would take fire in his own heart, and there would be no more distinction between "from that side" and "from this side." But, in fact, his life is filled by a duality that in no way corresponds to this principle. Certainly, he receives from all things and events a divine claim on his person, but in general no indication is thereby given to him as to what he should do for God in this hour, in this situation; rather, at most, so to speak, a question is directed to him that he must fill in with his own doing and not doing. What he now grasps, concludes, decides from out of himself, this he draws out of his "conscience," out of the primal awareness of his soul, at a depth in the source of unity of the person where self and world, and both in their present relation to each other, are examined and clarified. But no matter how powerful the concentration of the innermost forces, the conscience at no time has any certainty. This man knows, indeed, that he cannot know with objective sureness whether what he now has in mind is the right answer to the question posed to him, the right filling in of the circle that has been drawn. There are, certainly, hours in which he acts as with full authority, but also those in which he experiences complete abandonment, and between the two runs his life. He must allow himself to be helped: by the traditional "word of God," opening itself to him, so that the divine element in it can strike his soul, and by any good helpful spirit that has been touched by the spirit of God. But above all he must ask help of God Himself through offering Him in prayer all the fruit of conscience that He may accept it or reject it. And what if he has exhausted everything, and still he has won no certainty? Why, then, he must live through this hour just in risk, in fear and trembling.

Let us now set opposite this solitary and exposed man, as the most extreme example of a religious certainty, on whose horizons apparently no shadow of the autonomy problem can ever appear, a religious community (here it no longer makes sense to think of an individual) that lives in an unshaken and by all appearances unshakable certitude which is lent it by its living tradition, a certitude that has become a higher nature and supreme self-evident truth. Within its life, religiously defined as a whole, a religious sphere in the narrower sense, embracing cult and ritual, nonetheless defines itself for the men of this community and an ethical sphere opposite it. Common to both is the fact that their laws and rules derive from the divine authority, and action according to them or contrary to them stands under divine sanction. And yet there ever again prevails in the religious sphere in the narrower sense a tendency that in a certain way reminds us of the tendency toward moral autonomy, however far it is in content from it. One wishes to observe the customs of worship and the ordained life forms not merely because they have been commanded; one wishes the inwardness of one's own relation of faith to find expression in them; one wishes to perform them as acts religious by their intention and content, as acts religious in themselves; and the fact that they are commanded can thereby so far recede as motive that what is experienced in them above all is that the One who commands has shown men the way to express and to satisfy their own religious need to be near to God and to be ready for Him.

In the other, the ethical realm, a corresponding tendency prevails, in a different manner but at times with no less strong accents. It is commanded to honor one's parents; but for the respectful man an innermost reality from the ground of life manifests itself therein. It is forbidden to bear false witness; but to the upright man truth is not only the seal of God, but also the treasure of his own soul. It is commanded to love one's fellow men; but is love genuine when it does not spring forth in the heart? From above and from within at the same time: that just that which is commanded from above may well up from within as longing and impulse of the soul—that is the final aim of this tendency. In the measure in which the fire of God shining above men in infinite distance and majesty is enkindled in the innermost chambers of the self, thus, in the measure in which the "divine image" becomes concrete reality, the difference between heteronomy and autonomy is dissolved in a higher unity within the community living in the living certitude of the tradition. Only at this stage, where the religious principle has incorporated the ethical without injuring it in its own proper power, is its primacy incontestable.

But this is by no means the highest stage. For here, indeed, within the total life of the religious community there are still the two realms, the religious in the narrower sense and the ethical;

separated from each other in kind; both, to be sure, tracing themselves back to the command of God and related to it, but still each, if not in all its parts yet as a whole, claiming pre-eminence. But when a serious inner crisis has undermined the foundations—just the certitude that it is God's will that men live so and not otherwise—and a movement has arisen in the community in order to overcome the crisis and again establish a clear, unambiguous life in the face of God, then the separation between the ethical and the religious does not endure. For the new movement the ethical actions must become religious actions by their nature and their effect, thus not merely belonging to religion as being commanded by God but an inseparable ingredient of its germinal substance and throughout of no lesser rank than the rest, indeed of such significance that this rest, the "religious in the narrower sense," could not exist without it. The original intention of the religious community, the realization of "holiness" in the whole breadth and fullness of the common life, shall now be fulfilled; with it fulfillment is begun. The "ethical" is now no longer an affair between men authorized and sanctioned by the religious authority, but it is, no less than the religious in the narrower sense, an affair between man and God. Both types of actions, the ritual and the moral, are by their meaning directed to God Himself, through both the connection with Him is maintained, both help to effect the unity between the divine forces and forms. The isolated religious element has disappeared here even as the isolated ethical one. You cannot really love God if you do not love men, and you cannot really love men if you do not love God.

This is the stage that Hasidism reached, even if the new life established by it remained fragmentary and fleeting. One shall, says Kierkegaard, have to do essentially only with God. One cannot, says Hasidism, have to do essentially with God if one does not have to do essentially with men.

II For a spiritual movement which does not strive for the dissemination of a concept but the renewal of life, it is characteristic how its human ideal relates itself to the individual universally valued and prized human qualities. The Hasidic attitude is illuminated through the sayings of three zaddikim. These sayings are related to one another, yet each has a particular tone and makes a particular contribution; more than this, they indicate a clear line of development. These sayings are concerned with the relative valuation of three qualities: cleverness, piety, and goodness. Rabbi Pinhas of Koretz, a man of the first generation and one of great directness in view and speech, contented himself with erecting a scale of values for the three. "I prefer being pious," he says, "to being clever, but I prefer being good to being clever or pious." At first glance it appears as though the ethical is here placed above the religious; but if one examines the related concepts (in the original Yiddish) more exactly according to the former manner of speaking, then one marks that what is meant here by "pious" is the special religious, hence the isolated religious, in contrast to which "good" designates the man who relates himself with love to the world through seeking to fulfill the will of God for His creatures. The isolated religious attitude was, in fact, known to Hasidism in its own environment, in the form of devotees who were solely concerned with their relation to God Himself; but the isolated ethical did not exist in this environment, and therefore it was not at all taken into consideration.

A concise saying stemming from the school of Karlin, whose time of flowering falls in the third and fourth generations of the movement, goes further than this saying of Rabbi Pinhas. It reads, "Cleverness without heart is nothing at all. Piety is false." What is here called "heart" is at base clearly nothing other than that "goodness" without which all intellectual superiority is vain. The second part of the saying is astonishing in its trenchancy. What it wishes to say is clear: a direct relation to God that includes no direct relation to the world is, if not deception, self-deception; if you turn away from the world in order to turn to God, you have not turned toward the reality of God but only toward your concept of God; the isolated religious is also in reality the not religious.

Now, however, comes the third saying and lays bare the perversity of all isolated qualities while it also criticizes in noteworthy fashion the isolated goodness. For we are now in the sixth generation; the enlightenment movement has meanwhile brought to the Jews of Eastern Europe too a form of isolated ethic, and in addition the originator of the saying, the wise Rabbi Bunam, has also probably become acquainted with other forms of this isolated ethic in his foreign travels. The saying goes, "If someone is merely good, he is a profligate lover; if he is merely pious, he is a thief; if he is merely clever, he is an unbeliever. Only when all these qualities are together in one person, can he serve God in completeness." Whoever devotes himself to men with a vague love without order and form, without both faith and wisdom, without receiving through wisdom meaning and connection from his faith, it is easy for him to lose himself to one or the other like a profligate lover. He who wishes to limit himself to an emotional relationship to God, without seeing the living world around him and without knowing life, steals from men what is due them, and why not also, therefore, what belongs to them? And he who only exercises his mind and is intent on nothing else, he who is joined with God and the world only through the external bonds of customary inherited religion and inherited morality but knows neither piety nor goodness, will soon lose as well the scanty foothold that those external bonds lend him. Everything isolated leads astray. Only wholeness is reliable and leads man to salvation.

In so far as a scale of values is established in these sayings, the ethical is in the foremost place: he who is only "good" can more easily acquire what he lacks than he who is only pious or merely clever. We encounter a similar valuing of the ethical, though from another direction, where what is discussed is no longer the qualities as such, but the place of the love of God and that of the love of neighbor in the development of the truly religious person. Here it becomes fully clear that true human love in the eyes of Hasidism is by no means a detached ethical attitude but a religious attitude in the most proper sense, indeed that in the development of the person the religious itself can most easily be built just on this love. A zaddik asks one of his disciples, "If a Jew arises from his bed in the morning and has to choose in one moment between two ways, the love of God and the love of neighbor, which takes precedence over the other?" The disciple did not know. Then he explained: "In the prayer book it is stated, 'Before praying one shall say the verse: Love thy fellow as one like thyself!' The true love of God begins with the love of men. And if one should say to you that he has love for God and has no love for men, know that he lies." It should be noticed that, despite the saying in which mere goodness is condemned, still nowhere, as far as I see, is it said that no one can feel love for men without love for God: the former is always regarded as the foundation. Before a grandson of the "holy Yehudi," a zaddik of the seventh generation, a merchant brought a complaint against another who had opened a business next to him and reduced his profits. "Why," asked the zaddik, "do you attach yourself so to the business by which you nourish yourself? What really matters is to pray to Him who nourishes and preserves you! But perhaps you do not know where He dwells; now then, it is written, 'Love thy fellow as one like thyself, I am the Lord.' Only love him, your fellow, and wish that he too may have what he needs,—there, in this love, you will find the Lord." While elsewhere in the Scriptures one is commanded to love God and then the stranger because God loves him, here the converse way is indicated. Certainly both together are the truth: for each of the two loves in its truth demands the other for its completion and helps the other along; but it is significant that in Hasidism it is the way from the world to God that is ever again indicated as decisive for personal development.

We are taken a further step toward the understanding of this fact by a statement of one of the disciples of the Seer of Lublin, hence a zaddik of the fourth generation. It is a saying that seems naive, but in its naivete is hidden a deep truth. It too begins with the verse from the Hebrew Bible, "Love thy fellow as one like thyself." "For," it continues, "as when one first teaches the child the consonants and the vowels and then unites them into a word, so is everyone in Israel in truth a letter of the teaching and his soul a particle of God from above, and who loves one out of Israel attains a particle of God, and if he becomes worthy to love still another and still another, he attains more, and if he becomes worthy to love the whole of Israel, he attains the Almighty, the God of the World, the Lord." The real meaning of the saying proceeds from its conclusion: only he who learns to love one man after the other, attains, in his relationship to God, to God as God of the world. He who does not love the world can know in his relationship to God only a God who is solitary, as it were, or the God of his own soul; the God of all, the God who loves His world he first learns to know through himself loving the world. Thus one may then regard the way from love of man to love of God as decisive for the development of the person, not as though he had to go this one way and not the other. Rather the living man of faith must go both ways repeated times. Ever again his love becomes too narrow, one time on the one side, one time on the other, ever again he must widen and renew it. But that which is decisive for education is the way from "below" to "above."

One man came to a zaddik and asked, "I have heard that you give effective remedies. Give me then a prescription for acquiring the fear of God." The zaddik answered, "I have no prescription for acquiring the fear of God, but I have one for the love of God." "That is indeed a yet higher rung," cried the man, "just give me the prescription!" "The prescription," said the zaddik, "for acquiring the love of God is love for Israel. He who truly has love for Israel can easily come in addition to love God."

As close as the "ethical" is here to the "religious" in its fundamental significance for the latter, a difference of qualities and provinces still remains. This too must be bridged over. And it has been bridged over.

A zaddik of the third generation, one of the greatest from the school of the Maggid of Mezritch, Rabbi Shmelke of Nikolsburg, was asked by a disciple: "How can I fulfill the commandment, 'Love thy fellow as one like thyself,' if my fellow does evil to me?" He answered, "At times one hits oneself by mistake. Should one then take a stick and thrash oneself soundly as punishment? You are, in fact, one soul with your comrade, and if he does evil to you because he does not know this, will you, who know this, requite him in kind and thus do injury to yourself?" But the man asked further: "And if I see one who is evil against God—how can I love him?" "The soul of this man," answered the zaddik, "is a particle of God from above. So you should have mercy on God when one of his holy sparks has been imprisoned in the 'shells.' " Here the decisive step is taken. As the primal source of the divine is bound with all His soul-sparks scattered in the world, so what we do to our fellow man is bound with what we do to God. The "ethical" actions are by their meaning and nature just as much religious actions as the "religious." And if one asks about the result: one of the most serious Hasidic thinkers, Rabbi Joseph of Olesk, he too a disciple of the Maggid of Mezritch, writes, "So long as groundless hate exists, so that one person does not regard the other with a friendly countenance, it causes the concealment of the countenance above. But when love brings open countenances, then it is fulfilled that the glory of the Lord reveals itself and all flesh sees it together." Redemption depends on the unification of the human world, for this unification is the unification of the divine substance that has been cast into the world. The genuine moral act is done to God.

Thus it is self-evident that the "ethical" actions should be compared with the "religious." The Seer of Lublin, for example, when he himself served food to a poor wanderer and also himself brought out the eating utensils, answered the question why he took so much trouble over the matter: "Bringing the utensils out of the Holy of Holies also belongs to the service of the High Priest!"

If one might still understand this as mere parallelism and speaking in simile, then the innermost unity of both spheres and the religious character common to both is expressed in an almost uncouth jest of Rabbi Mordekai of Neshiz, one of the early zaddikim. He had pursued a business in his youth and used all through the year to lay something aside from his earnings in order to be able to buy a beautiful etrog* at the end of the year. On the way into the city where he wanted to look for one, he met a water carrier who wept and wailed because his only horse had perished. The rabbi gave him the money that had been saved for the holy purpose in order that he might buy another horse with it. And when he was asked whether it had not been hard for him to make such a sacrifice, he said, "What difference does it make? All the world says the blessing over the etrog, and I say the blessing over the horse that has been bought!"

A God who so truly takes part in the destiny of His creation that He separates Himself from His Shekina for its sake and makes the reunification with it dependent upon the unification of creation, cannot tolerate—so teaches Hasidism—that in his life and actions man should make a fundamental distinction between above and below.

* A citrus fruit, or citron, over which the blessing is spoken on Sukkot, the Feast of Booths.

III

It remains to show by several sayings and stories how this integration of the ethical into the religious finds its expression in the exercise of love for man in the life of the true hasid. Some among them remind one slightly of older stories, but what is in question here is not the individual saying but the fullness and strength of the whole, which is without comparison.

We start from the view that we have found in that simile of Rabbi Shmelke about the man who hits himself. It is a principle of identification not unworthy of being placed by the side of the Indian *tat twam asi* ("Thou art that"). A saying goes back to the Baal-Shem-Tov himself who again attaches himself to the command to love one's fellow "as one like thyself": "For each one in Israel has his roots in the Unity, and therefore one may not thrust him away 'with both hands,' for he who thrusts away his comrade, thrusts himself away: he who thrusts away a particle of the Unity, it is as if he thrusts away the whole." As illustration, I set next to this saying a forceful, popular parable that stems from the school of Rabbi Yehiel Mihal of Zloczov. This parable also clothes its forcible admonitions in jesting form. Again a man complained to a zaddik that another destroyed his gains. "Have you ever," said the zaddik, "seen a horse drink at a brook? It strikes out with its hoofs. Well, why this? It sees its own reflection and thinks that it is another horse that wants to drink up its water. But it is given to you to know: that is no other than yourself, you yourself stand in your way!"

The intense demand of identification is thoroughly compatible in Hasidism with the insight into the special character of the relationship of each man to himself, but also the problematic peculiar to this relationship is clearly recognized. Just on the basis of this problematic the command of love has gained new aspects. I cite two sayings that seemingly stand in a certain opposition to each other but in truth supplement each other. The Baal-Shem-Tov explains the command thus: "It lies upon you to love your comrade as one like yourself. And who knows as you do your many defects? As you are nonetheless able to love yourself, so love your fellow no matter how many defects you may see in him." But a zaddik of the fifth generation said of himself: "How can I fulfill the command of love since I do not even love myself and cannot bear to look at myself? What do I do? I execute the turning so fully that I can again look at myself. Just so shall I do to my comrade." Here two men of different stages stand over against each other. The one does not let the knowledge of his own inner frailties hinder him from turning to his person the loving attention seemingly natural to men; to the other the sight of his own soul, as it is, is an insurmountable obstacle to loving himself; he can only overcome it through purifying, changing himself, through "turning"—a concept, incidentally, that is already highly characteristic for the fusion of the ethical and the religious in an early historical development of the Jewish tradition. Does this mean that he cannot love the imperfect at all and therefore also not his fellow men until they have completed the turning? But it is, in fact, still clear that it is just through love that he helps the others to turn, instructs and counsels them therein. The deeper significance of the sayings is rather that the zaddik who through true turning to God in addition brings himself to love himself in God, that is, in the perfection, can also help the man who entrusts himself to him to love him in the same way, hence in truth, instead of, as ordinarily, in the deceptive perspective of self-seeking.

Here love already begins to pass over from the realm of the personal relationship between man and man into the relationship to the community. What the zaddik works in each individual he works in the structure of the whole. "And this is the work of the candlestick," quoted a master of suffering and prayer in the fourth generation, the Kosnitzer Maggid, from the prescriptions for the manufacture of the implements for the holy tabernacle, "a work of gold from its base to its flower." And he expounded: "The zaddik shall cleave to the totality of Israel and also to the faithless, 'so that no one who is cast off be cast off by him'—from the beginning to the end, to the lowest of all, all one work and completely united, and the setting right shall happen to all, for each is a divine particle from above." Each "setting right" that the zaddik exercises on the individual, he exercises on the totality of Israel. It first is the true candlestick which shines up to heaven and illumines the earth.

From this conception of the totality, which recurs in Hasidic literature in innumerable teachings, parables, and personal examples, a characteristic view is to be understood that already emerges in all clarity in the first generation and was not further developed later. It is the idea of "loving more." Proceeding from the Baal-Shem, it then found a footing with Rabbi Pinhas of Koretz and in his school. It is reported of the Baal-Shem that he had bidden a hasid whose son had fallen among the atheists to love him more than before and this loving more had in fact brought the youth back to the community. And to Rabbi Pinhas is traced the teaching: "When someone despises you and does you injury, you shall strengthen yourself and love him more than before. Through such love you will bring him to the turning. Therefore one shall also love the evil, only their evil deeds shall one hate." And Rabbi Pinhas' most genuine disciple, the man of whom it is told that death came over him in a night when he lay on the floor and could not decide either to give evidence against another before a court or to speak the untruth and saw no other solution than death—Rabbi Rafael of Bershad—used to teach: "If a man sees that his companion hates him, he shall love him the more. And the meaning of this is: the whole of Israel is a carriage for the holiness, and if love and unity is between them, then the Shekina and all holiness rests over them, but if, God forbid, there is a rupture, then a rent and an open place comes, and the holiness falls downward into the 'shells.'" When, therefore, at the one place there is too little love, at the other one must love so much the more in order to create agreement and restore the wholeness of the "carriage." The lower world bears the divine only when it holds together as a whole, and each can contribute at his place to the wholeness being preserved. And the same principle of loving more reaches in its effects into the intimacy of inter-human life. A disciple of Rabbi Rafael tells: "On a trip in summer the rabbi called to me that I should sit beside him in the carriage. 'I fear I shall make it too crowded for you,' I said. Then he said to me in an especially affectionate manner: 'Let us love each other more, then there will be room enough for us.' " The feeling of being too crowded in the human world has its origin in insufficient love.

What counts, however, is no general, impersonal love; it must be wholly concrete, wholly direct, wholly effective. Perhaps no other example says so directly what is meant by this than that well-known story that has been handed down from the mouth of a great lover and helper, Rabbi Moshe Loeb of Sasov. He himself is supposed to have told (I select among the different variants in circulation the most popular and complete) how he sat among peasants in a village inn and listened to their conversation. Then he heard how one asked the other, "Do you love me, then?" And the latter answered, "Now, of course, I love you very much." But the first regarded him sadly and reproached him for such words: "How can you say you love me? Do you know, then, my faults?" And then the other fell silent, and silent they sat facing each other, for there was nothing more to say. He who truly loves knows from the depths of his identity with the other, from the root ground of the other's being he knows where his friend is wanting. This alone is love.

And how does one attain this? One must bow down low to one's companions—so the Baal-Shem taught in a badly preserved parable commenting on the verse of the Proverbs of Solomon, "As in water face to face, so the heart of man to man"—as if one wished to come near his reflection in the water and bowed down low to it, and it too comes to meet him until his head touches the water and he sees nothing more, for both have become the one that they really are; so the heart of man comes to man, and not this one to this other alone, but all to all. Thus Moses, the "humble," bowed himself down to the "level of the ground" and love for one another entered the heart of Israel. From another side and likewise calling on the humility of Moses, this same view is presented by an early zaddik of the third generation. Each man, so he teaches, was more important to Moses than himself. "And this was his service, to bring Israel too to this stage so that each should love his companion through being inferior in his own eyes and his companion superior to him. . . . And this is the meaning of what is written: 'When Moses lifted his hand,' that is, his strength and rung, which was the quality of true humility, then in Israel too there was the quality of humility, and then each considered the superiority of the other and his own inferiority and loved his companion in perfect love, and by this they vanquished Amalek," that is, the power of evil.

And again the ethical enters wholly into the religious. The "holy Yehudi" and his friends loved to draw an analogy between two Jews (Yude) standing side by side on an equal footing and drinking to each other in joyous love with the connection between two "Yud"—Hebrew letters. The Yud is the smallest sign in the Hebrew alphabet, indeed a mere point, yet if one places two of them next to each other, then they express the name of God. If, on the contrary, you put two such points on top of each other, then all they signify is an interruption. Where two stand side by side on an equal footing and are open to each other without reservation, there God is.

Before this great significance of being on an equal footing one to the other, the differences in value between men fade. Not only is there in each man a particle of God from above, in each there is one unique to him, not to be found elsewhere. "In everyone," says Rabbi Pinhas, "is something precious that is in no other." The uniqueness and irreplaceability of each human soul is a basic teaching of Hasidism. God intends in His creation an infinity of unique individuals, and within it he intends each single one without exception as having a quality, a special capacity, a value that no other possesses; each has in His eyes an importance peculiar to him in which none other can compete with him, and He is devoted to each with an especial love because of this precious value hidden in him. Certainly, there are great and small, those rich in teaching and those poor in teaching, those adorned with virtue and those seemingly bare of virture, those devoted to God and those who have crept away into themselves, but God does not deny Himself even to those decried as foolish and as wicked. Rabbi Pinhas compares this to a prince who in addition to his majestic palaces also owns all kinds of tiny, out-of-the-way cottages in forests and villages that he visits at times in order to hunt or to recuperate. And it cannot be said that the great palaces exist by right and not the tiny cottages, "for what is effected by the unimportant cannot be effected by the important." "So too the righteous man. Certainly, his virtue and his service are immeasurably great, and nevertheless he cannot effect what the evil man effects." So every man who wishes to walk in God's way must avoid making absolute differences out of relative ones. The statement of the Mishna, "Despise no man," is extended by the Kosnitzer Maggid (who quotes that parable of Rabbi Pinhas) not merely to the ignorant, but also to the evil and the vulgar. For, as the Mishna says, "there is no man who does not have his hour." "The evil man too has his special hour where he turns to the Creator," even if he speaks to Him "only one single word in perfection," "for not as chaos did He create him." If in the life of the most evil this moment did not exist too, he would not have been created at all. And it is for this moment, this one holy word, this one holy action that God looks. How can man forget that! In his readiness for love and help he may not be fastidious where God is not so. It is told of the Sasover Rabbi that about midnight as he was absorbed in the study of the teaching, a drunken peasant pounded on his window and demanded entrance. At first the zaddik was vexed by the disturbance, but then he reflected: "If God can bear him in His world, if it is indeed necessary that he be there, then I must also bear him in my world." He let him in and prepared a bed for him. Another time someone reproached him for giving all the money that he had to a man reputed to be bad. "I too am not good," he said, "and God gives me what I need."

God lavishes his love even on the most wicked; how then can man administer his own love with strict bookkeeping according to honor and merit! Once the Polish rabbis met together in order to sit in judgment over those who had become disloyal to Jewish customs. But before they proclaimed to the world their verdict separating "those who throw off the yoke" and the faithful, they decided to ask Rabbi Wolf of Zbaraz, also one of the great lovers, for his assent. "Do I then love you more than I love them?" was his answer. The proceedings were not continued.

"The perfect zaddik," teaches the Baal-Shem-Tov, "in whom there is no evil sees no evil in anyone." Thus it is reported of Rabbi Susya, the great ecstatic and "fool of God," that even when one did something evil in his presence he saw in him only good. According to the legend, he reached this stage because once after he had angrily asked a habitual sinner, in the presence of his teacher, the Maggid of Mezritch, why he was not ashamed to step before the holy man, the Maggid had blessed Susya henceforth to see only the good in all. According to another account, his attitude was such that he perceived all sins of others as his own and reproached himself for them.

For him who is not a perfect zaddik, the Baal-Shem-Tov gives the supplementary teaching: "If it happens to anyone that he sees something sinful or hears of it, let him mark that in himself there is a small particle of this sin, and let him make it his business to set it to rights. . . . For the evil man too will accomplish the turning if you include him in the unity, since in fact all men are one. Then in addition you will cause it to turn out according to the saying 'and make the good,' for you make good out of evil." Here Jewish wisdom of faith meets from a wholly other side with the ancient Chinese: He who brings himself into unison with the meaning of being brings the world with him into unison; but here, in the Hasidic saying, stands what is lacking in all Taoist ones: One must include the other in the unity, then one has a good influence on him.

One must guard oneself before this eternal distinction between oneself and the other, before this arrogance of distinction, before this whole triumphal world of illusion built upon a self-satisfied distinction. Nothing so disturbs the unity of God's world, the foretaste of eternity, as this swaggering distinction between myself and the other as though I really excelled in this and that over one person or another. The most extreme statement in the sphere of speech that Hasidism has uttered against this high tide of false distinction is what Rabbi Rafael said when he believed death near: "One must now lay aside all good works in order that there may be no more separation of the heart from any Jew."

But there is still one category of men whom it is especially hard for us to love; these are our enemies. The attitude one should have toward this love has been expressed by another great zaddik, also one of the first, Rabbi Yehiel Mihal of Zloczov, likewise before his death. He commanded his sons that they should pray for the well-being of their enemies. "And do you suppose," he added, "that this is no service of God? This is a greater service of God than all prayer." Here the integration of the ethical into the religious has reached its peak.

IV Hasidism is one of the great movements of faith that shows directly that the human soul can live as a whole, united in itself in communication with the wholeness of being, and indeed not merely individual souls, but a multitude of souls bound into a community. The realms that are apparently separate from each other by necessity recognize in the exalted hours of such movements the illegitimacy of their reciprocal delimitation and fuse into one. The clear flame of human unity embraces all forces and ascends to the divine unity.

The unification of the ethical and religious spheres as it has been accomplished in exemplary fashion in Hasidism, even if only in a short-lived flowering, brings forth what we, in our human world, call holiness. We can know holiness as a human quality hardly otherwise than through such unification. It is important to come to know it.